Yidumduma Bill Harney was born on Willeroo Station in Wardaman country in about 1936. Like most Aborigines of that time, he was born bush, under a paperbark tree. After a traditional upbringing, he became a stockman, and eventually head stockman. In between times he was a saddler, a mailman, a windmill rigger, a pine cutter, a poddy dodger, a crocodile shooter, and a fencer. A successful claimant in one of the Northern Territory's early land claims, he is now an artist and tour operator, concerned to share his knowledge and culture, from the Land of the Lightning Brothers, with both black and white people.

Jan Wositzky, a writer, storyteller and musician, was born in Scotland in 1951, and his Czech-Scots family emigrated to Australia in 1956. He fell in love with traditional celtic bush music, and in 1970 co-founded The Bushwackers Band. Later he wrote books such as the bestselling biography of Tommy Woodcock. His interest in the Northern Territory began with a stint as a fettler on the old Ghan railway, and for the last decade Jan and his family have travelled extensively throughout the Northern Territory, performing, making television documentaries, and writing a stage play, 'Bilarni', based on the life of Yidumduma Bill Harney's father.

FROM THE LAND OF THE LIGHTNING BROTHERS

BORN UNDER THE PAPERBARK TREE

A MAN'S LIFE

TOLD BY MASTER WARDAMAN STORYTELLER YIDUMDUMA BILL HARNEY

Written by JAN WOSITZKY

an
ABC
BOOK

Funded by the Australia
Council for the Arts

Published by ABC Books for the
AUSTRALIAN BROADCASTING CORPORATION
GPO Box 9994 Sydney NSW 2001

National Library of Australia
Cataloguing-in-Publication entry
Harney, Yidumduma Bill, 1936?– .
  Born under the paperbark tree: a man's life.
  ISBN 0 7333 0514 8.
  1. Harney, Yidumduma Bill, 1936?– . 2. Wardaman (Australian
  people). 3. Aborigines, Australian – Northern Territory –
  Biography. I. Wositzky, Jan. II. Australian Broadcasting
  Corporation. III. Title.
305.89915092

Designed by Kaye Binns-McDonald
Cover photographs by Jan Wositzky
Map by Geoff Morrison
Set in 11/12½ pt Bembo by
Midland Typesetters, Maryborough, Victoria
Colour separations by First Media, Adelaide
Printed and bound in Australia by
Allwest Print, Perth WA

5 4 3 2 1

FOREWORD

This is Bill Harney here, and I'm going to talk a story about Aboriginal life.

I am an Aborigine who was operating in the early days. When I was a kid I listened to the stories that were passed from my mother's grandparents to my parents. From my Aboriginal stepfather, old Joe Jomornji, I learnt the full Aboriginal culture, the Aboriginal way, in the bush. I learnt proper Wardaman language. I know the names of all the trees, grass, tobacco, fish—everything. I can sing ceremonies, and I know Aboriginal law.

Then later I moved across from the Aboriginal camp to the European camp, and on the European side I learnt a lot. I became a qualified stockman and a supervisor in the stock camp. If we delivered twelve hundred or fifteen hundred bullocks to the drover, no worries at all, I can count them just like that! And I got all this knowledge on my own accord.

Now, today I am a painter, and I take tours to Wardaman country, Bill Harney's Jankangyina Tours—to the Land of the Lightning Brothers, and we camp out there near the rock paintings and I give people the history of the country from the olden times. I've got a very good mind and a good brain to remember right back. Not like a lot of the young fellas today who know nothing. You can tell them the history and they forget within two seconds. But not with us, all my brothers and sisters—we've got the stories—it's built in our system somehow. When we start talking all the words fall like a snooker ball in a hole, or like water from the roof falling into the ground.

Anyway, my white father, old Bill Harney, he wrote a

few books, and it started to build up on my mind to make a book of my own. Probably his spirit flew straight across the land and over my mind. 'Before I die,' I said, 'I must put something together so the whitefella who came from a long way away might be able to get a good run-down of what life was like in this country. I'll just try,' I said. 'Might be an interesting book.'

But I couldn't do the book myself because I haven't been to school to learn to read and write. But a friend of mine was Toni Bauman, and she was Adult Educator at Barunga, an Aboriginal settlement south east of Katherine, and I used to talk to her a lot. 'I might tape some stories,' I said. 'Might be you are able to help me to put a book together?'

Toni turned around and said, 'Can you tell a good story?'

'Oh too right!' I said. 'I gotta lot o' stories!'

'All right,' she said, 'I'll buy some cassettes and you tell the story.'

This was back in 1979. I was working out at Amanbidji Station—just operating the bores and doing up the saddles, doing a bit of mechanics and running the houses, and flying around in the air all day with the helicopter, mustering cattle and yarding them up—and when we come home from the cattle work in the afternoon to the homestead I used to pick up my cassette and drive off to where no one was making a noise. I used to sit under the tree and tell the stories by myself, talking to the cassette. Some time a big breeze would take my voice away from the cassette, so I used to get in the car and wind the glasses up on each side, and I'd stay inside talking my head off—talk, talk, talk, talk all the way. The only time I stopped was when the tape ran out. I talked so long I had a sore arse! And then one day my missus come along and said, 'Boy you must be crazy to talk like this!'

But I just went on and fifteen tapes I filled up, and then one afternoon I went over and saw the manager's wife in the homestead and I said, 'You want to listen to the stories that I told? We're going to write a book.'

She said, 'All right,' and she shoots on the cassette. 'God!'

she said to me. 'I could sit up and listen to that all day. It's a very interestin' story you're telling.'

'Well, this is what I heard,' I said, 'and what I seen, way back, since I was kid.'

YIDUMDUMA BILL HARNEY

CONTENTS

PREFACE

As a storyteller, Yidumduma Bill Harney is a man for the nation to cherish—a rider on a never-ending track of stories, cantering out of the past into the present.

I became involved in the process of turning Bill's tapes into a book in 1987, when I was researching a stage play on the life of Bill's father, the famous Northern Territory writer and storyteller W.E. (Bill) Harney (1895–1962), I was introduced to 'young Bill Harney' in Katherine, and was initially surprised at his existence because he was not mentioned in his father's books, and W.E.H. was generally open about sexual relations with Aboriginal women.

The reasons for this lack of acknowledgment are given in Yidumduma Bill's story, but I was attracted to Bill because, like his father, he's a top storyteller. I was lucky to gain a love of storytelling as a boy listening to both my Czech and Scots relations, who all like to talk a lot, and storytelling has, ever since, been my favourite way of getting information.

When I first heard what was on the Amanbidji tapes, however, I was flummoxed by Bill's stories, all related in a light-hearted manner, of a land where there was so much violence and physical pain, morally outrageous by present standards in Australia, but apparently commonplace on the cattle stations of the north during the first half of this century.

These shocking stories were lightened by ripping yarns of characters such as opium-smoking drovers—respected Territorians all—who under cover of the Second World War carried out cattle-duffing escapades, but it was still a foreign culture to anything I'd been taught at school, or seen on a television screen.

Like nearly all of us who were educated in Australia, particularly coming from 'down south', I knew precious little about our historical relations with Aboriginal people, and in my ignorance was shocked to read that, for example, poisoning of Aborigines with strychnine still occurred almost into my lifetime.

This sense of culture shock was deepened because, compared to most of what I had previously read about Australian Aborigines (which was written by non-Aborigines), there was in Bill's Amanbidji tapes a reversal of roles, with 'them' recording 'us' instead of the other way around. And as I listened, I had a growing sense of being like the explorers who were unaware of the tribespeople watching them pass.

Bill's stories, however, were about everyone else in the country, and there was very little about Bill himself, and so this book is the result of the Amanbidji tapes plus two more taping sessions focussing on Bill's personal life—ten-day sessions under shady trees in and around Katherine and Ingaladi Waterhole.

I have tried where possible to locate written accounts of the incidents Bill talks about, but many of the events in this book appear to be unaccounted for elsewhere, or for reasons of time I have not been able to locate them.

In some events, such as Bill's father becoming a ranger in 1957 at the then Ayers Rock–Mt Olga National Park, Yidumduma Bill has a sequence of events different from the facts in his father's account. But Yidumduma Bill's recounting holds a version of a truth held by many people—that the national park was established because W.E. (Bill) Harney went there, rather than the other way around.

This story is an honest account of an honest life, told so as to share that life with us all. As with all our personal stories, its truth lies in the insights that a list of facts cannot hold, at least not without the interference of a flesh-and-blood storyteller.

Since the recording sessions my job has been to transpose Bill's language and story onto the written page so that people without previous contact with Aboriginal stories will find the book a pleasure and an education, while at the same time the story remains deep enough to engage those who are already interested in this area of history.

While I am Bill's servant in this book, and my role is to be the vehicle for the telling of his story in his own way, my influence on the work is inevitably significant, particularly in its structure. Given this impact of collaboration, I hope, on the page, that I am as silent as possible. The stories in the original Amanbidji tapes were told in Western narrative style, and remain so in this book. Also adhered to is Bill's Aboriginal way of using English, and for the novice reader one of these ways needs explanation.

Aboriginal people Australia-wide often refer to females as 'he' instead of 'she'. However, possibly because Bill was of European as well as Aboriginal heritage, and is, as he says, going 'both ways', he uses 'he' for 'she' occasionally, and it's in the book as Bill spoke it on the tapes.

Also, when Bill talks about family, please note that in Wardaman and other Aboriginal systems of kinship, which are classificatory, one's father's brothers—uncles in the European way—are classified as one's fathers. Likewise the sons of your father's brothers—cousins in the European way—are classified as one's brothers. It is also worth noting here that, in acknowledgment of his European audience, Bill Harney calls his mother's Aboriginal husband, Joe Jomornji, 'stepfather' (Bill's biological father being a European man), and so he also refers to Joe Jomornji's brothers as 'stepfathers', whereas in Aboriginal company he would simply refer to Joe and all his brothers as his fathers.

The final part of the process was for myself to read the manuscript to Bill for his amendments and approval. During the time we have worked together on this book it has been striking that while these stories speak of much conflict between black Australians in their homelands and white Australians on their frontier, the teller of these tales is a man equally comfortable with both his Anglo-Celtic and Wardaman heritage. To me it seems that ease is the basis of a successful life that continues to grow and prosper in many directions.

But it is only recently that I've come to realise that Bill's achievement is greater than it originally appeared, because now, having spent some time working with Yanyuwa, Garrwa, Mara and Kurdanji people in the Borroloola region of the Northern Territory, I have seen just how uncompromising the system is to Aboriginal sensibilities, and witnessed that while governments are willing to spend many dollars on Aboriginal organisations, very few schemes are designed to educate black Australians as to how the system actually works, or to give them a chance at fair-dinkum empowerment.

Having also noticed that real empowerment is often not supported by the general public, it seems to me that any indigenous Australian who battles his or her way through this morass of obstacles and succeeds in life is a hero. In this context Bill is a living symbol of what Australians are trying to achieve by our present reconciliation process—that is, peace between black and white.

On a personal level, Bill's story is universal to males the world over, and a classical model for any man of any age to contemplate: childhood with mother, initiation by older men from youth to man in both the European and Wardaman worlds, followed by the working man's long slog to establish himself and, with the development of his skills and fortitude, the realisation of himself, in his own business, with family, continuing his Dreaming, and husbanding the generation to follow.

As our professional collaboration grew into friendship, it's been an honour for me to know Yidumduma Bill Harney and, as Bill said to those who grew him up, I say to Bill, with great respect, 'thank you, old man', for the opportunity of recording this story.

JAN WOSITZKY

ACKNOWLEDGMENTS

In the first instance, this book owes its existence to Toni Bauman, who in 1979, whilst Adult Educator at Barunga, responded to Bill's desire to write a book. Toni supplied a tape recorder and cassettes, and had the original tapes transcribed. She has also been involved with all the subsequent steps, and without her initial interest and continuing supervision in seeing this project through, and her friendship, this book may never have been.

This book was also made possible by funding from the Australian Institute of Aboriginal and Torres Strait Islander Studies in Canberra, the Aboriginal and Torres Strait Islander Arts Board of the Australia Council for the Arts, the Northern Territory Tourist Commission, the Northern Territory Arts Council, who also donated office space and use of computers and printers, and with funds from the Northern Territory History Award 1994.

We extend a big thank you to all the above for this generous support, with a special mention to Chris Burchett and Ray Scanlon for their particular interest, as well as Bob Maza, Marcia Langton and Ted Egan, for their recommendation of this project.

The documents in this book are gathered from the archives of the State Library of the Northern Territory, Northern Territory Archives, the Australian Archives, and the Katherine Museum. To the staff of these institutions—particularly Michael Loos, Jenny Amour, Jenny Wright and Greg Coleman—thank you for pointing us in the right direction. Thanks also to my friend Fiona Duncan for additional research.

For kind permission to reprint from the writings of W.E.

(Bill) Harney, many thanks to Ruth Lockwood.

The exacting and time-consuming job of transcribing the cassette tapes was done initially by Noelene Hicks and Linda Law, and later by Katrina Sporton and Glenys McInerney in Victoria, and Pauline Schindler of the Northern Territory Archives. To these skilled people, thank you for a fine job, and thanks also to Frances Good who facilitated this process with the NT Archives.

Many thanks also to Peter Menhennit of Montrose, Victoria, for transferring information from IBM to Macintosh systems.

As there were many names of people and places that the writer was unfamiliar with, assistance with spelling was required from people who know this country. For giving information that was not on the printed map, many thanks to Russell Young and Tex Moar of Pine Creek, and Debbie Bird-Rose, Pearle Ogden and especially Darrell Lewis, all of Darwin. For assistance with historical details, many thanks to Northern Territory historian Peter Forrest.

For assistance with the spelling of words in Wardaman and other Aboriginal languages, we are grateful to the Katherine Regional Aboriginal Language Centre and to Denise Angelo in particular. However, as languages are a living thing, we cannot be certain that these spellings are definitive for all time, and acknowledge that future Wardaman linguists may amend any inaccuracies and inconsistencies in this text.

Creative projects such as these invariably involve the assistance of friends. For beds and swag space, many thanks to Andrew McMillan, Margaret Egan, Bob Elcoat, Ray and Rowena Scanlon, and especially to Ken and Julie Barnes, who welcomed Jan into their Katherine home and introduced Bill and Jan to each other.

Last, but certainly not least, appreciation is due to our families, especially to Debbie Sonenberg, who, when these projects were under way, carried the extra burden on the home front for Jan.

PART ONE

CHILDHOOD (1936)

Chapter One

THE DEVIL-DOG WITH HORNS

My father, old Bill Harney, was a white man, but I was grown up by old Joe Jomornji, my Aboriginal step-father. We were living in the caves in the escarpment country on Willeroo Station, which is about 120 kilometres from where I now live in Katherine town, and Joe taught us how the old Aborigines painted the first white man they saw when he come to this country on the horse, about two hundred years ago. Old Joe Jomornji said his grandfather's father saw the first lot of white men, with the guns, and so they painted the man with the gun on the wall of the rock.

According to old Joe, it took the old Aborigines a long while to realise who the white man was, because for us the devil in this country looks like a white ghost, and they thought the white man was a devil. Then when they saw the white man riding a horse they thought he was riding the devil-dog. And when they saw the cows with the horns, they reckoned it was the devil-dog with the horn on it, and they whacked the cows onto the rock. 'Wow!' they said. 'We must spear this devil because he's got the devil-dog!'

Then other Aborigines said, 'If we spear that ghost, the devil-dog might chase us,' and they were frightened, and they ran away to the banks of the waterhole, ready to jump in so the devil-dog wouldn't catch them.

Joe told us how Captain Cook came into this country and brought the white man and the laws and the cattle, and put them in the land to start up all the cattle stations. 'If Captain Cook never come, no white man would have ever been in this country'—that's what Joe said.

When the first lot of white men came into this country,

they saw a huge number of Aborigines. But they wouldn't just go close by and try to talk to them, they just fired a shot or two to get into the waterhole, and so they started shooting the Aborigine. This killing, I think it started over the Queensland side and gradually worked over this way, and it's been right through the Territory.

When we were kids, the old Aborigine was telling us that if the European had never fired any shots, and just come to catch a lot of Aborigines from the bush to become a working man, well, that would have been all right. But the white man just saw the Aborigine and he said, 'Oh they only blacks, we just bowl 'em out quick, get rid of 'em.'

So some Aborigines swung back and were saying, 'How we gunna get on with them, because they are shootin' too many people 'round here?'

Then the Aborigine saw the white man riding along and said, 'We know. He gotta go that way. We'll meet him in the other end and we get him.' Of course the European bloke wouldn't be expecting an Aborigine hiding in the scrub with the spear, and he'd be busy riding, and of course he was knocked off the horse with the spear. Sometimes they'd follow him right up to the camp, and when he finished having his tea he'd be laying around doing nothing, and they'd go close by and hypnotise him, and walk close up and knock him off with the spear. This was the story from Willeroo, where I was born.

One man they killed was Mr Scott. He was the first white man at Willeroo, back about the 1880s, and he was at a place called Old Willeroo, not where that new fella homestead is today. Old Joe told me that while he was in there setting up this place he heard lots of noises on top of the escarpment where the Aborigines were living. He was a little bit worried about his cattle and he headed across there, and he thought the Aborigine was no good and he started firing a shot at the old Aborigine, and they cleared over towards Delamere way— that's the station next along from Willeroo, still in Wardaman country—and some of them said, 'Oh we must go back and kill him.' When they went back across to Old Willeroo, Mr

Scott wasn't there at all. He was across at a place called Rocky, and they went across and speared old Mr Scott at Rocky.

Then the Aborigines were knocking off quite a few of the white man that was squatting down on their land, and the European was saying, 'Well there's so many Aborigines 'round here spearing Europeans, might be shooting is the only one way we can settle it out, or maybe we could poison them out.'

Old Johnny Durlu told me about this getting the wild blackfellas in from the bush, and the poison. I was a kid, and he was an old man about seventy to eighty when I knew him, and he used to sit down and talk to me. He was the first one that the pioneers caught and brought in, and Mick Madrill, he was the first European over in Delamere, and when they settled at Delamere they went out in the bush there and they shot a lot of Aborigines. They yoked a chain over old Johnny's neck, then took him over to Delamere with the other old blokes. They worked them in the homestead to build the yard, and after they finished building the yard they went to have lunch and they gave them curry and rice and a bit of bread. But the Europeans had put strychnine in the lunch, and some of the old blackfellas died. It was lucky for old Johnny. 'When I seen all the others fall arse over head,' he said, 'I raced up and I got a handful of mud and put it in me throat and brought it back out. But some already died.'

After that they never forgot, the yarn was spread all over. They said, 'If you get flour from white man, don't touch it, leave it.'

But some decent European blokes thought another way: 'We might be able to pick up a couple of young fellas from the bush and train them up to talk English, and then send them back out in the bush to talk to the rest—to tell them out in the bush that the European doesn't want to do any harm to him, just want the land to operate the cattle, and that they can come into the property and work.'

So they picked up some Aborigines and taught them a bit about the cattle, and they sent the Aborigine back out in the bush and to talk to the rest: 'This mob, white man here,' they said, 'he's going to start up a place to put all the cattle here, for something to eat, and we want to go over there so we can work in the station with them. I gotta take youse over there to where the white man is with the cattle, and then we'll all sit down and he feed us, and you get to know all about it.'

Then they gave the Aborigine a feed of beef and when the Aborigine had a taste of the beef they reckoned it was great. 'Well,' they reckoned, 'maybe the European gunna do the right thing? Maybe they not gunna shoot Aborigine any more, and we'll forget about spearing them, and then a friendship might start that way.'

So the young fellas come in to work on the station. They were taught to make rope, they were taught to make hobbles, to break in a horse, and how to control the wild cattle. They were taught how to brand, and about camp-drafting and night-watching cattle, and moonlighting waterholes for wild cattle.

But then the old Aborigine that was still out in the bush started spearing the cow, and the pastoralists were picking up lots of cows with a spear stuck in the jawbone. That's the time they rang the police and said, 'You must go over in the bush and collect all the Aborigines and bring them in for us, if you don't mind, because they're spearing a lot of cows.'

We were told about this from my old granny, old Wayingarring. My granny got kidnapped from the bush and brought to the white man's side. They said to her, 'If you don't show us where the Aborigines are hiding, we'll shoot you. If you show us, we'll give you a feed. If you don't, we'll starve you all the way.'

So my granny was riding a horse and she used to show the police the place where the Aborigines were living. She took them down at the back of Deep Creek and all around Jibber-man Gorge, and when she showed them where the blacks were, they used to shoot them. At first she thought they were just going to pick them up to work on the cattle station, but they used to sneak up to them first thing in the morning, gallop over with the horse, and open up on them with the revolver. When she saw they were shooting them, she said, 'Doesn't matter if they shoot me, I'm gunna run away.'

She was telling me she took all her clothes off and made a special type of boots out of emu feathers so they couldn't trail her, and she took off bush, and she turned up where our mob was with no clothing and these emu feather boots, and she told them about it. 'They killed quite a few in the family,' she said.

Then these policemen rode right down to the escarpment country, and they heard all the Aborigines there and they said, 'Well, we've got them all cornered, what we do with them?'

'Gallop across with the horse and then jam them in and make sure they don't all get away.'

But the Aborigine was up on top of the escarpment on the lookout point, and when they saw the cloud of dust coming they gave a hoy from the top and sang out, 'Someone coming with the pack-horse!'

Then the main mob who speared all the cows disappeared in this little tunnel. The policemen galloped right into the camp and bailed the others all up. They said, 'We've got youse all now, we're not going to let you go. You stay still, and one bloke can put the handcuffs on all of you.'

The policeman put handcuffs on everybody and he searches around the camp site. All he can see is the crocodile bones and turtle shell. The policeman can smell the beef, but he can't find where the meat is. He can't find any carcass of any sort because the carcass was buried under the ground, real deep, and they've got a camp sheet on top of the ground and they're all sitting on it. Of course the policeman wouldn't have brains enough to lift him up and start digging underneath him.

They question the Aborigine, 'Youse all here in the bush spearing the cow?'

The Aborigines say, 'No, we don't spear any cow, that belong to the white man. We only kill our food—emus and kangaroos.'

'All right,' he says, 'I believe you. We'll go down and look another place,' and the policemen rides away.

Then as soon as the policemen was gone the old Aborigines painted the policeman in the rock, with the clothing and big sombrero hats on, and the big revolvers, along with the devil-dog. Some other times the policeman took away the young fellas in handcuffs, and then the old Aborigines painted a mob of them naked Aborigines with handcuffs on. Old Joe told us that the policemen brought them back to the homestead, and gave them a talking to there, and so the Aborigine come to be a working man. We worked for the white man then.

> After Scott was speared Tom Pearce took up the lease on Willeroo. [Tom Pearce is accredited as Mine Host in Mrs Aeneas Gunn's classic *We Of The Never-Never*.] In 1907 he built a six-roomed house, kitchen and pantry, and erected a branding yard at Willeroo.
>
> From 'Station Profile', written by National Trust NT for *Katherine Times*, 20 June 1985

My stepfather Joe Jomornji was working for Tom Pearce, along with an old grandfather of mine in the Aboriginal way, old Harry Huddleston. They told me Harry come down with the horses and Tom wanted Harry to muster all the cows, and Harry said, 'Look there's a big monsoon rain coming, we can't muster that cow.'

Tom said, 'No, we got to get this cow off to send them away.'

Harry said, 'Okay, we'll go ahead,' and he packed everything and went out mustering, and the big rain come in. All the rivers were flooded, and Harry told me himself that on the north side of Ingaladi waterhole the really big rain caught them up. They couldn't move. Everywhere you went there was a big bog. They were on this little high mound that was the hardest place they could find, packed up like sardines, with the horses and the cows and everything. Around was water everywhere, and they were sitting there, sitting there, and they ended up letting all the cow go, and Harry said, 'I'll try and walk back and get some food because everything's wet now and we can't eat anything.'

Old Harry ended up walking back to the station, and

when he got back Tom Pearce said, 'What are you doing? Where's the cows?'

He said, 'You can't bring the cows because everywhere is flooded.'

Tom said, 'Oh well, I won't have you any more. You must go.'

Lucky Harry had his horses there, and he went over and said to old Tom, 'Could you give us some tea and sugar, and a bit of flour for the road?'

But Tom wouldn't give it him. 'You can go and starve,' he said, and old Harry packed up and went.

Of course Harry was all right because he could get the bush food. Then one time Tom Pearce had lots and lots of horses in the yard, and there was a small storm, and there was a bloodwood tree in the yard, and the lightning hit this blood-wood tree, and killed all the horses at the same time, about seventy horses, and Tom Pearce made up his mind and said, 'Hell! I'm going away,' and that's when Vesteys come in.

> Vesteys were a multi-national consortium of private companies with widespread interests in beef cattle, controlled by an English Vestey family. The group was started in 1897, and by 1916 had acquired 93 239 square kilometres of land on pastoral leases in North Australia, including the 538 square kilometre Willeroo, purchased in 1915 from Tom Pearce. By 1926 Vesteys were the biggest leaseholders in the Northern Territory.
>
> From Peter d'Abbs, *The Vesteys Story*,
> Australasian Meat Industry Employees' Union, Victorian Branch, 1970

Vesteys is a huge big pastoral company. He owned half of the property in the Northern Territory, a third of the property in Queensland, and 50 per cent the property in Argentina, that's what Vesteys owned. They made Holbrook's sauces and Imperial sauces. They had a big huge office in London and in Sydney, and I was born on a Vesteys station, and I was reared on a Vesteys station, and I worked on a Vesteys station, at Willeroo.

That's my country, Wardaman country, and it's full of beautiful scenery with lots of tabletop mountains around the top of the escarpments, where you can see for miles over the black-soil flood plains, all covered in bush foods and medicine, and with Aboriginal tools like spear points lying around all over the place from the old days. And there are many different places where there are red and yellow and orange ochre in the rocks, and spinifex and trees—all sorts of trees, coolibah, white gum, some baobab trees come in from over Western Australia, and the paperbark trees all along the water channels that run into the Flora and the Madison river. We've got this land back now with the land claim, and soon we'll be going from Katherine town, back to my country, where I was born and grew up.

Chapter Two

BORN UNDER THE PAPERBARK TREE

I was born in about 1936, at a place called Brandy Bottle Creek, away from Willeroo homestead, under the paperbark tree. None of this hospital business. There was never any doctors—just one old lady who was like a sister, and she watched the kid as he was born. The only time the men went across there was if the kid was crossways and couldn't be born. Then one special old operator, he'd sing that kid inside a woman's stomach—it's a very secret song, I can't sing it to you—and next thing the kid would start to move and twist around till he was right way. Of course the mother would be still screaming, and he'll be singing, and then when the kid is coming the sister lady would come in and say, 'All right,' and that old boy used to get up and just stand away and just give his back, and he'd call, 'Everything okay?'

She'd say, 'Yeah, that's all right,' and the old boy would walk away then and the kid would come out. Then they rubbed very soft dust all over the baby's body, and they would drop the baby in this little coolamon—like a bowl made out of a sapwood tree or a paperbark—and this special old lady cut the cord with this little stone knife.

That was a fantastic and neat way they did it, and that's why I can't work out today why they go for the operation. Might be they have the operation because in the hospital the Aboriginal lady is in another world to her own system, and she gets a little bit shamed, and frightened to push it out or scream with a doctor standing there, but it's not like years ago when I was born in the bush with old Aboriginal singer and the old ladies together.

My mum was Ludi Yibuluyma, and she was a nice old lady—she died not long ago when she was ninety-three—and after I was born my mum was working on the roads with my father, old Bill Harney. When I was a young boy I asked my father where he was from, and he said he was born in Queensland. And another old bloke was telling me that he was a friend of old Bill, and he said they jumped the boat that come across from London to Australia . . .

W.E. (Bill) Harney had fought in the First World War, and later told his story in an ABC radio program titled *Harney's War*: '. . . gradually I felt a hatred for war and what it stood for. And a hatred for discipline and what it stood for. So when I come back to Australia, I got off at Melbourne and I went straight through . . . and I met some old mates of mine on the Georgina River, right back where I'd started from. Old Andy was there and we had horses and away we went. I rode eight hundred miles to Borroloola on a horse, to forget about it all. When I got back to Borroloola, I saw the blacks there . . .'

From *Harney's War*, ABC Radio, 1958

. . . the next thing they got mixed up with the old Aborigine. Old Bill lived with them, having a drink, and they were feeding him the mangrove worm. Then he saw the Aborigine fighting and throwing spears. 'Thought I got away from the war,' old Bill said, 'and there's a war on over here amongst the blacks!' The spear was flying and they're dodging the spear, and my old man said, 'Over there at that other war we can't dodge a bullet because we can't see 'em comin' and a bloke can get shot straight away. But here,' he said,' the Aborigine is fightin' and dodgin' a spear.'

I said to a chap that was there, 'Look, I don't see any wounded layin' about this place, and they're all fighting with spears.'

'Oh no, they've got a different way,' he said. 'When two men fight among the Aborigines they have umpires. The umpires are their godfathers. They jump in between and they talk and explain the whole thing to one another.'

And I said, 'Well blimey! That's a good way. It's like top-level talks, it's a form of arbitration.'

'Oh well,' he said, 'war is a strange thing. It's passed down through the ages and one day we'll overcome it. We'll just get like the old blackfellas, I suppose, and talk things over and everything will be peace. But until then we've got to educate ourselves.'

From *Harney's War*, ABC Radio, 1958

Anyway, he hooked in with the old Aborigine, and he worked right through in the coastal area, right down to Darwin district and he finished up around Bathurst Island and he got tangled up with another old lady from that side. She was Linda, and she was different one from my mother, and my brother Billy from Linda was born before me.

> Bill Snr married Linda Beattie, an Aboriginal inmate of the Emerald River Mission on Groote Eylandt, in 1927, while a trepang fisherman in the Gulf of Carpentaria. They had two children, Beattie and Billy. By 1932 Linda and Beattie had both died of tuberculosis. Bill Snr then put his first son Billy in a home in Townsville, Queensland.

Jan Wositzky

I only met my other brother Billy once when I was little, because later he drowned in the Todd River in Alice Springs. Anyway, after Linda and Beattie died, old Bill Harney came out to my country to make the road through Willeroo, and that's the time he run into my mother. He saw my mum Ludi, and my grandfather old Pluto, and he said to them, 'Would you like to come work with me?'

Pluto said, 'All right,' so old Pluto, and Minnie my old grandmother, and my mum, went making the roads with Bill Harney. They showed him the way right through from Willeroo to Victoria River Downs Station (VRD). My grandfather used to go along in the lead and blaze the trees all the way, following the old Aboriginal walking pad, and old Bill would come along behind him making the road. They call it the Victoria Highway now, but it was never the Victoria Highway at all—it was just the original Aboriginal walking trail right through Arnhem Land and Katherine Gorge and past Willeroo, right down to Western Australia. They used that walking trail to trade their boomerangs and spears and many different ochres, and when they did the trade they had ceremonial meetings.

That had been a walking trail for a hell of a long time, and then the first lot of drovers ever to come into the country used the Aborigine as a guide. The Aborigine showed him the waterholes, all the way from Cape York right through Borroloola and straight across the country. They hit Roper River and followed the Roper River all the way past Mataranka— there was no Mataranka that time, there was just the river— and they came right past Willeroo.

Then after the old Aborigine showed the drovers the way through, the cattleman said to one old Aborigine called Brumby, 'Well, Brumby, you know your way to Willeroo, could you make a track?'

Old Brumby said, 'Yes, I'll go ahead.' He yoked up one hundred donkeys to his wagon, and he pushed a two-wheel track right through from Manbulloo—that's just out from where Katherine town is today—to Willeroo. Then from Willeroo on to VRD, old Bill Harney made that road. If old Bill and Pluto come across a big ditch, a lot of other boys used to get a flat rock like a concrete slab, and they used to get the anthill and crush that up with grass in a bucket to wet it, and mix it up like a cement and ram him in the cracks. Today that road is bitumen, and that is unbelievable because in my time it was only just a two-wheel track, and when she started to rain you couldn't see the two-wheel track at all. But you can have a look on Delamere Station today, and those crossings are still there—the floodwater never washed them away.

My mum was the cook, making damper and johnnycake, and looking after me at the same time. 'We used to put you up on top of the wagon,' she said. 'You always had a sleep there, while we went on ahead makin' the road.'

'Oh,' I said, 'I didn't even know I was there.'

'You were there on top of the wagon,' she said.

I said, 'Jeez, I had a long ride then, eh? All the way from Willeroo to VRD.'

According to old Pluto, my grandfather, we were with old Bill Harney for about four years—that could have been from 1933 right up to 1937. Old Bill Harney and my mother had a girl before me—Dulcie Harney—and I was the second after her. Old Bill Harney treated them all right; employing them, but with no wages. There was never any money. Old Bill used to clothe them and feed them, and old Pluto was happy to get his shirt and trouser and a bit of feed. He was laughing, you know, and children worked with no clothing. We were happy to get a little bit of bread and beef.

When old Bill Harney finished making that track he left us. Bill wanted to go carting stores with Burt Drew. Burt Drew was the donkey team man, and the donkey team is a hundred donkeys pulling a wagon with a long chain, and the big wagon would carry from 40 to 50 ton. Old wagon driver Drew and Bill Harney were friends, and they were off carting stores to all the places around the bush; from the depot at Timber Creek right through to Victoria River Downs, then down to Wave Hill over to Catfish (Hooker Creek—now Lajamanu). That's about 200 miles. They would only do about 5 or 6 mile a day, about 10 kilometres, and it would take them maybe four weeks to get there, but they would just plod along until they get there. These days the donkey runs wild, and people are very nasty to the poor old donkey, they go around shooting donkeys, but the donkeys carted all the beds and everything else for the people, and ploughed the road with the old fire-plough—there was no grader in that time.

Anyway, then old Bill was 'Donkey Team Harney' and he was away with the donkey team. My mum wanted to stay there with me to keep me and my sister Dulcie under control, and that's why they split up, and then my mum come in to live at Willeroo homestead.

Chapter Three

TOP LADIES

That's when was I growing up on the cattle station. There would have been about a couple of hundred Aborigines around the homestead at Willeroo, all Wardaman people, and we used to build a humpy for ourselves. We used to split a lot of little kerosene tins in half with a stone axe, and that was our galvanised iron. Then we went out and cut little trees down and put up a forked stick and then nailed the kerosene tin onto the stick, and so the kerosene tin would hang on in a big storm. If we didn't have a roofing nail we used to just cut up a lot of fencing wire and make a point on it and bend the end like a head. You've got to have about a thousand kerosene tins to make a humpy out of that sort of thing, you know.

My mother was with old Joe Jomornji now. Joe had been working with us on the road with old Bill Harney, and he was my Aboriginal stepfather. But my name was still Harney, like my mother. Her Aboriginal name was Ludi Yibuluyma, but they still called her Harney, and that's why myself and my sister Dulcie took the name of Harney. See, in those days Aborigines took a second name from the European bloke they were with, or the one they were working for, and my mum was Ludi Harney, even though she was with Joe Jomornji. From March to October old Joe Jomornji was in the stock camps with Pluto, my grandfather, and I was at the homestead with my mum and old Minnie, and all the other Aboriginal women who were working on the homestead.

Old Minnie was teaching my mum to make homemade soaps, and how to milk cows—the 'cow shepherdess' they used to call them—and a lot of them used to make homemade butter. Another woman was the goat shepherdess, and she used to look after the goats, and they all did a lot of washing-up and ironing of clothes with the metal iron heated up on a wooden stove. One old Chinese man, Eric Kim Sing, was the gardener when I was a kid, and he used to teach the Aboriginal ladies to grow everything—carrots, tomato, pumpkin, shallots, turnips, rockmelon, watermelon, some tomatoes and cabbages and all this sort of thing in the garden, just to keep the property going. They cut lots of little drains and made irrigation channels with their hands, and they used to carry a lot of water and fill all these little gutterings so you could grow all the vegetables in this garden.

Sometimes us kids used to creep down there picking the vegetables, and the Chinaman was sitting down with a shotgun—he didn't have lead in the shotgun, just a handful of sulphur in the shell—and he would see us coming, and watch us bending down and picking up the carrots and, 'Youse gunna get a shotgun up the arse,' he'd say, and then he let this shotgun go, and didn't that sulphur hurt in the backside! Oh Jesus! We never looked back—we kept running and we never pulled up till we were back at the homestead, and we were hiding!

Anyway, those Aboriginal women did a wonderful job for the property owners. A lot of them would be out in the field picking up conkleberry bush and nutwood tree to make a broom, and they made the place look real clean. Those trees are good too for some tucker, with the beautiful blue grape off the conkleberry, and a peanut from the nutwood. Anyway, then all the ladies got stuck into pulling up all the weeds and long grass around the property and around the homestead. Minnie, my grandmother, she was cleaner in the house—she was the 'big house girl'. The 'big house' is the homestead where the big nobs would be eating. The Aborigine would always eat in the woodheap, and the working European and the part-Aborigine, they always went over to eat in the kitchen, and my mum worked in the kitchen. That's where the old cook was, and the old Aboriginal ladies always carried the meat and stuff on the tray over to the big house so the white manager and his wife could eat.

When they were having a meal us kids used to always go down to the dining room and pull the punka—the punka is a fan hanging from the ceiling—and we used to cool them off. We were doing it to get some custard. When they finished their meal, any left over they used to give it to us, and we used to eat it in a little corner there. We loved it. We reckoned that was great. The homestead used to supply us once a week with the tea and sugar and a bit of beef, just to keep us going. No wages. And we was happy, and everybody was happy. The dollar coin or the two bob piece, we wasn't interested, because he wasn't ours at all.

Then you'd see a string of old Aboriginal women, with a tomahawk and their swag straps on their shoulders, going out to get a load of wood for the kitchen. There was no motor car in those times, and they used to walk for 3 miles, about 5 kilometres, and carry heaps of wood over their shoulder tied up with the swag strap, like a row of camels walking in a line, and we used to follow them. We used to get a little swag strap and tie a little firewood up and bring it back to the kitchen too, and we stacked the wood up in the woodheap place—enough wood to last the cook a fortnight. Then when the cook was short of wood they had to go out again and get another load.

I was only a little boy and I don't know, but I heard that sometimes old Bill Harney would come back with Burt Drew and the donkey team, and they used to come up to Willeroo and say hello to my mum, and they would help with this snigging in the wood. They'd go out with a donkey team and the old wagon and they'd bring a big load in. Then of course from October to March the wet season would come in and the donkey team would get bogged, and old Bill Harney was away somewhere else, and the wood would run out, and the station would get all the old Aboriginal women again, with a swag strap over their shoulder, and a tomahawk, and away they would all go to get the wood.

Then the cook would cook up a meal, and the women would boil up the clothes in the boiler and do the washing-up, and some old women would make homemade soap. If you're telling the young fellas today that we had homemade soap, they'd say, 'What's that?' but it's made out of bullock fat. We used to boil the old bullock fat and put caustic soda in it and tip it over in a big tub and leave it set over night. Next morning you go along and cut it with a knife, and it was proper soap. They used to wash clothes all right. Oh Christ, it was good! You wash your hair and everything with it. But after a while I think Aboriginal people got blind because there was too much caustic, and with the caustic all around your lip of course you get poisoned a little bit. Apart from that, the old Aborigine had their own soap. It was a white wattle leaf, and we used to use that for soap out in the bush. But when you come into a station, of course you used this homemade soap.

Now, looking back to the old people and what they did for the white people, well, they worked for them hard—they used to go and go and go. And those old women they were happy-go-lucky, and after they did that wood carting, they used to go out every day and pick up loads of bush food, and come back to the camp and did all the woman's ceremonies, and everyone was happy in those times. They were top ladies.

Chapter Four

COCK-RAG AND SPEAR

When all the ladies were working around the station, Joe Jomornji and all the men were out mustering cattle in the stock camp, and in that time there were lots of old Aborigines still living out in the bush. Joe knew where they were, and when he was working on the cattle, he wouldn't take the European bloke to where they were. The white man didn't know the country, and Joe'd be going the opposite way to keep the bush people under cover all the time. Sometimes when I was a kid the bush people used to creep into the homestead—but only in the night, not during the day—and see us if they needed a bit of tobacco. We used to always give it to them, and bread and meat for them to eat, and they'd bring in the bush tucker. Then they'd be gone, living on the escarpment. The last old fellas died in the bush around about 1951. Some would have been around about the eighty mark, and they never worked at all for the station, they just explored in the bush all their life.

Anyway, Joe was out there working the cattle from about April on, and then in October when the wet season was coming on, Joe and all the other men would come back to the homestead. The cattle work knocked off for the year and all Aboriginal people used to give up their boots and trousers and put them back in the store on the station at Willeroo. Everybody would take the shoes off the horses, grease all the neck straps and saddles, and store them in the saddle shed. If it was a shirt they were wearing, the shirt was left in the store for next year with the stock work. This was the Wet now, and from the store we got a tarpaulin and mosquito net, and off we'd walk out in the bush dressed up with only a cock-rag—that's a little *narga*, like underpants, and you cover yourself on the front and the backside.

I'd grown up a bit bigger now, and I was walking around with a cock-rag and little spear—we always went out with a spear. Wherever we went there were still Aborigines in the bush. We were around Ingaladi waterhole, where my tour camp is now today—that was the big main base camp for the Aboriginals. There was a huge number of them living on the river along there where the cave painting is with the policeman and the devil-dog and the gun, and they were living down at the Flora River as well.

Anyway, if it was wet we used to live under the caves in the hills, and when it was dry we'd be down the river camping out in the fresh air under the trees. My old grandfather Pluto looked after me in the bush, and he taught me everything. He carried me around in the bush all my life, showing me how to catch goannas and porcupine, and also how to catch emus and kangaroos. Along with Ludi, Pluto and Joe really taught me everything in the bush.

Joe Jomornji taught me about getting fish by poisoning the waterholes with the bark off a gutta-percha tree—milkwood. We drop the sap and the bark in the waterhole, then you wait a quarter of an hour. The bark goes down in the water and the fish think it looks like red meat coming down, and snap at the bark. But a milk explodes out from the bark and the milky sap stings the fish in the eye and the fish just go berserk. They go real mad! They come up in the air to get away, and I've seen a big barramundi shoot out of the waterhole onto the mainland and kick away everywhere and buck back into the water and take off again. Crayfish! I've seen them walk out of the water because of the sting in their eye.

Then there's a kapok in the rocky country. It's similar to a corkwood tree. It's a very soft wood, and he has a very stringy bark on him, and we used to peel all the bark off that tree, leave it dry, then crush it all up, then wet it, and just roll it with a hand to make it like cotton and have a fishing line.

Then we had a hook made from a special little wattle tree. A very hard wood he is, and we would grind him on the rock and put the curve around him and make a little point—just enough to tie this little string on it. We used to put a grasshopper on the end of it, and throw it in the water, and that way you'll catch a fish.

Then we went diving into the deep water, picking up turtles from the caves in the water, and now and again we'd come across a crocodile—only the freshwater crocodiles, none of these saltwater crocodiles. Then one of us will pop up and say, 'There's a crocodile here.'

The others would say, 'Well get him.' Then there'd be two persons dive down in the water, and one bloke would put his hand underneath the crocodile's jaw, and put his thumb over his eye to make sure he can't see anything. Another bloke will grab his tail and kick away from the bottom to bring him up near the top.

The others waiting on the bank will say, 'You got that crocodile?'

'Yeah, I got him 'ere. Youse got the rocks ready?'

'Yeah, we got the rocks ready.' Then they used to get a vine off the kapok tree and put it around his snout, and bring him up to the top—but hang on tight to his hide—and on the land they put a flat rock underneath his jaw, and one other bloke with another goolie, the bigger stone, hammered his head and squashed his head to pieces. And that's the way we got our crocodile, and cooked him up in the ground oven. That way he tastes like chicken, but if you fry him, he tastes like a fish.

Then Joe Jomornji and Pluto used to show me how to make a spearhead out of a rock, and how to make axe heads. That old grandfather of mine was a bugger because he wouldn't use that European axe—he had to have his own special axe, the stone axe. If any Aborigine had the steel axe he had to have stolen it, and if any of the older fellas saw a young fella walking around with the steel axe he'd say, 'Oh you gotta take that axe back. That belong to the white man. Take 'em back, don't touch that. Because if white man sees it we'll all be going to gaol.' They were frightened of everything. 'Don't touch any white man gear,' that's what they were saying.

Anyway, they showed us how to make the axe heads and the spearheads. First we used to get the big rock and roast him in the ground like a lump of meat, and leave him overnight. The next morning you pull this hot rock out of the ground, and when you hit it it just splits straight away, and we used to make lots and lots of spearheads out of the rock. When the spearhead was still warm, we used to bury this spear point into the wet sand from the river. That way you'll bring all his strength back and make him go hard again. Then with Joe Jomornji we always went out hunting with the spears, for kangaroo, emu, and then us kids we used to go out hunting ourselves. But now today, all the young fellas, you can't teach them at all—you can, but they don't want to leave the town.

Anyway, when the storm time is coming on, the porcupine comes out of his hole and starts digging up the anthill for ants—when it's dry he can't get his nose in to get the ants because the anthill is so hard—and we used to pick up a huge number of porcupines. First off we put him in a red-hot fire and just turn him around a few times and pull all the spikes off his back. When he was clean we used to cut him in the belly and throw all the guts out. After that you just stick two or three big rocks in the hole in the tummy, then put your porcupine into this little hole in the ground and put a paperbark on top of him and cover it up with hot ashes from the fire, and leave it roasting for about a couple a hours. Then you pull him out and there he is—cooked! Number one! Very little skin, but full of meat out of his leg and his arm, full fat, like a pig, but good eating. You won't stop eating! It tastes like ant because he lives on ant.

Then for our 'chicken' we used to make a bird trap out of a rock wall, like a barbecue in a circle. It was big enough to stand up in, with a little hole to get in, and we used to stand inside and make a roof with a few sticks and put some grass on top. Then we light a little fire outside and get inside again.

Then there's the smoke going up in the air and all the birds will swarm down to have a look at the smoke. You're inside and you've got a little stick with a feather on the end of it. You put this feather stick through this little hole in the roof, and when the birds see this little feather flying up and down, up and down, like a bird diving in and out in his burrow, then the birds come down to see what's going on there.

Well, you got a little rail across the hole so a bird can sit on it. Before he comes down you hide the feather stick inside, and the bird comes down to see where this little bird disappeared to. Well they're looking around while sitting on the crosspiece, and the old Aborigine will look up and grab the bird by his foot and pull him down and break his neck.

As soon as you take one bird, all the other birds will follow him—they think he's gone in there to get a feed, see. Another bird will come down to land and of course you take him, and another thinks that he's gone in there to get a feed, and he'll come down to land and again you grab him. You get about forty to fifty birds, no problem; grey chicken hawk, brown chicken hawk—we call him frog-face eagles—and kite hawks. They're all good eating, and this was how we used to live in the wet season.

We always know the wet season is coming on when we see the flowers on the paperbark and the white gum, in October, and we call that time *ngurruwun*, when the hot weather comes. That time is hot and dry in every way, and that's the time we went out to start hunting around for food. That's the summertime, and that's the time for the circumcision of the young boys.

Ngurruwun goes through to November when there's a big thunderstorm all around, and the old people say, 'Well, this is the wet season.' We call the first storm time *iudul yanarri*. Then all the fruit will come on the trees, the green plum.

And after that the big rain comes, and we call that *yijilk*, and we lived off the bushland, did all the big ceremonial dancing, and made lots of woodcraft like the old people showed us how to make. Then the knock-'em-down rain used to come in, the big winds that push over all the long grass from the rainy season, and the Aborigines from the bush will say to us, 'Well, you can see the old grass is all laying over. The wind is coming from the north, from the eastern side, from the south side, from the west side, knocking down all the grass. This is the last rain. We all go back now. This is the working season started.' And when we went home, sure enough, the month was March, and we went back to work on the station. We'd come back to the store at the homestead, and of course you put the mosquito net back in the store again for the next Wet. Then they give you a blanket for the winter to keep you warm, and a big army coat, and in the dry cold weather time we worked with the cattle and around the homestead again.

PART TWO

THE SECOND WORLD WAR
(1939–45)

Chapter Five

THE ARMY? FANTASTIC!

Then when I was at Willeroo, the wartime with the Japanese came along. I must have been about six or seven then, and I found out about it when old Joe and Harry Huddleston—my grandfather in the Aboriginal way, he was half-brother to Pluto—they used to take some cattle from Willeroo into Katherine town, and I'd run along with them, all the way, 70 mile. Willeroo were supplying the army with meat, and they used to bring the cattle into the army abattoir at Manbulloo Station—that was owned by Vesteys too. We had to have a pass to get past the provos guarding the road at Bunjari, but we were all right because we had the bullocks for the army, and we went through to Manbulloo.

Anyway, when we first ran into the provos on the road, that's when I heard the war with the Japanese had started. Soldiers were everywhere: in the Manbulloo area, at Willeroo, Victoria Highway, and Delamere, right down to Victoria River Downs. They had camps all around in that country, right down to Western Australia. The road that old Bill Harney had made was made wider with the convoy trucks driving along, mainly blitzes. Wherever the cattle stations were, the army camped there too. Anyhow, the army saw the old Aborigine with the spears and boomerangs, and they reckoned, 'What's that?'

Old Harry Huddleston was there—they used to call him 'Livery Huddleston' because he was always in shithouse moods, he wouldn't talk to anybody—but anyway he said to the army, 'Oh, this is a boomerang we have a fight with, and this is the type of spear to get emus and kangaroos.' Then they showed the army how to throw the boomerang, and the army reckoned that it was ideal to fight the Japs.

Then the colonel said to Harry, 'How you stop the boomerang?'

Harry said, 'We'll show you. I'll stand up over this side and Joe Jomornji will stand up on the other side. You watch this now. He's gunna throw the boomerang at me to kill me, and next I'm gunna throw another one back to Joe.' Old Joe started and he threw the boomerang at Harry and Harry stopped it with the shield. And Joe went flat out because when Harry stopped it, the boomerang snapped. Then old Harry threw one back at old Joe Jomornji, and he stopped it.

Then the colonel said, 'This is ideal, all right, that's great. Can we buy some off you?' I was sitting down there and I saw the army bloke put his hand in his pocket and pull out a red ten-bob note. We were looking at it, and of course Harry Huddleston didn't know what money was, he didn't know what to do with it. Then lots of the army came around to the camp and they bought a big mob of boomerangs off the Aborigine—ten bob a boomerang. But the old Aborigine didn't know what to do with the coins, and the army explained to them about the money. 'You buy something with this,' they said. Well, back then for that you could buy gaberdine trousers and a shirt and twelve tins of tobacco, but we had nowhere to buy anything—we had no shops.

Then gradually someone crops up with the idea that they can gamble on the cards with all these two-bob pieces. They played *gunjimab* and they gambled the coins over and over for years and years, and the money never went away. Now today with the cards in *gunjimab* you win lot of money, but back then the same money would come back and they could play all day. They reckoned it was great.

Anyway, the army bought all the boomerangs and there must have been easy four or five hundred army blokes living in the area, and every morning about nine o'clock they would be all saddled up in this exercise place, and they would salute one another. Next, the colonel or whatever he was would split them into two lots. He would put a couple of hundred over this side, and a couple hundred on one other side, and he would have them all fighting with the boomerang. Of course they couldn't stop it with the shield and some of them was getting hurt, and so they got some more information from Harry and Joe, and they taught them to throw these boomerangs. All day they was going, fighting with these boomerang. Then they went home and had a cup of tea, and they come back out in that open flat again, and went on throwing boomerangs.

I remember the army people saying, 'Might be the Japs gunna take over this place, they might push right across. Look out, you might have a Japanese boss 'round this country yet. But if they do come here, try to do something to 'em.'

The older boys reckoned, 'Well if they come here, we'll sing their bullets and stop their guns from firing a shot. Then we can finish 'em off with a spear.'

The army bloke reckoned, 'What you mean you can stop their guns firing a shot?'

Then old Harry and Joe Jomornji told the army that they could sing all sorts of songs—songs to make a sweetheart come back, and songs to make a sweetheart go away, and songs to kill another man. Secret songs. And the old army blokes are listening to them, and old Harry said, 'Just like we got secret songs for singing while we're making a boomerang. That song is called *yarrindi*, and that song is like a poison and it makes that boomerang a deadly weapon, and it flies well. If it hit you, it will kill you for good.' The army bloke was just listening to Harry and Harry said, 'And same way we got songs to stop the bullet in the gun. If you sing a rifle, the bullet won't go off— she just sticks in the rifle.'

The army reckoned, 'Yeah? That's great! We might take youse down to New Guinea and sing all the Japanese bullet.' Well, I don't know if they sang that song for the army blokes, but they wouldn't sing that secret song for us kids because we wasn't initiated. We believed him, but I never seen it.

Then the colonel said, 'What about the spear, you better show us the spear now.'

Old Harry and Joe said to them, 'We can't give you any spear because you might get speared.'

But the army asked them again, 'How you throw the spear? You grab it in the middle and throw it?'

'No, no, we got a woomera here.'

'What's a woomera?'

Harry said, 'It's a stick with a hook on it, and you hook the spear on the end, and it's like you got a extra long arm.' See, they get the *gijiwa* tree, the corkwood tree, and they cut it up and they make a woomera out of this to throw the spear with.

So old Joe and Harry were throwing the spear and the army was saying, 'Might be this is the ideal one for them Japanese. When you're firing a shot they can hear you, but with boomerang and spear you can get up close by and just hit 'em over the head with it.'

Anyway, all over the country they were training up with the boomerangs and the spears—but the spear wouldn't have any metal on the end of it, it was just the ordinary blunt one, you know. But oh, they hit one another! And heaps of soldiers, millions of them, took spears and boomerangs for fighting.

Then when we walked into Katherine with the cattle, we went to Manbulloo, just out of Katherine, and the army was also based around the back of Manbulloo, and you had to come in through there with a pass. At Manbulloo Station there were many Aborigines working there, and one day the army was canoeing around the river, and some of these army said, 'Let's go over to the blacks' camp and see if one of the boys can get some black girls for us,' because they needed it. Anyway they went across and they saw this old bloke sitting around the woodheap, the wood chopper, and they said, 'G'day, what's your name?'

He said, 'Shilling.'

They said, 'Oh yeah, nice to meet you, Shilling. Could you find a woman for us?'

Old Shilling said, 'Yeah, I can go down and tell them for you.'

The army said, 'Okay,' and they all sat down waiting for him.

Old Shilling comes back on his own and one of the army blokes said, 'Where's the woman?'

Shilling said, 'Wait yet. They'll come after.'

And they were waiting and waiting, and one of these army was getting very anxious and said, 'Go back and tell them to hurry up.'

Old Shilling goes back and was stuffing around there and he comes back and said, 'They not ready yet.'

One of these army blokes said, 'We can't wait any longer,' and all these army talked among themselves and said, 'We'll scrap this bloke and root him up the backside.' Anyway, one of them grabbed old Shilling, another one took the strides off him and knocked him down, and old Shilling felt the dick on his arse and he jumped up and took off with no clothes! Flat out right back to the camp! And he turned up there with no clothes on. The army cleared out because they thought he'd gone back to tell the manager of Manbulloo, old Tom Fisher, and old Shilling never come back to chop any more wood because he knew the army might be 'round there. See, man to man on the sexual side, there was none of that sort of thing with the Aboriginal, because there's a law against that. If they caught a man going with another man they'd get speared over it.

Anyway, the army was fantastic. They were in with the Aboriginal, more or less, and we made it up together, and the old Aboriginal always thought the world of them. If any army got lost bush they'd go on a real hunt for him, find him, and bring him home. And they really looked after us—tinned meat, Sao biscuits. Oh Jesus! We used to get them in bags full. Matter of fact, we used to go down to their kitchen and they used to just give it to us, and a tin of bully beef, and we all reckoned that was great. In that time we never saw lollies, tin of fruit, nothing—only the dried apricot. Apart from that, we never had anything on the sweet side. Anyway, they supported the Aborigine, and the Aboriginal treated them like they were their mates. They'd give us everything, and we was happy.

Then old Joe Jomornji and my mum Ludi had a little boy, David, and one time early in the morning my mum was there boiling up a billy and this plane came straight over, very low, and they said, 'Look out, the Japs comin'! We better take off!' It was a Lincoln bomber plane, but we thought it was the Japs flying straight over at tree level. Everyone was running to get away and someone hit this boiling billy of hot water and tipped it over David—he was only about six months old—and of course when the billy tipped, the hot ash and water just spread right over this little brother of mine, and he got scalded and he died. Well, he was only a little one, and he didn't know anything, and I was scalded too, and we went away and hid in the scrub for a couple of days because we were frightened of that plane, and then we crept back and got some medicine for where I got scalded.

So again, the war, to us, it was a very sad life, too. We didn't worry much. We didn't care whether we got bombed or not, because it was everywhere, more or less. We were all hiding in the bush, and we wouldn't keep any fire alight at night because they reckoned the Japs might fly over and find the fireplace and drop a bomb, and we all knew nothing about the war. They said, 'Japanese come across now, they fighting at New Guinea.' That's what they told us. I didn't know much till in 1953 I was sitting down at Willeroo with an old boy called Davy Croft, and he was telling me about it.

He said, 'When the army was in this country, we was taken away and put in army camp.' Old Davy was telling me that they went down to Darwin, and they're sitting down there one day at the army barrack place at Myilly Point, and the next they heard these flights coming, and they looked over and there was a row of aeroplanes coming, and the first thing that old Davy saw was that a big boat got sunk.

The Japanese planes went along and they bombed all these boats up the harbour, right up to the boat landing at the jetty. All the salt water was just lit up in a fire. Old Davy was telling me this plane come along real low, and this American soldier was saying, 'The Japs can see us sittin' down.'

Davy said, 'Couldn't you shoot 'em?'

'No, no.'

'Go on, shoot 'em, shoot 'em!'

The American was saying, 'If we shoot 'em they might swing back and shoot the whole lot of us.' Anyway they didn't shoot any of them, and the planes bombed the post office in Darwin, and the big machine gun bullets went through every-. where. When you looked up through the roof, there were holes like the stars shining in the sky.

And everyone—all the army and the Aborigine and the white man—they all just left their houses and headed up to the bush, into the scrub. They all said, 'We'll stay still here, quiet, don't move.'

The Japanese bombed Katherine too, and my first wife's uncle, old Roger, got bombed there. His son, Don Jambarlirli, often told me how they lived in the caves out near the Katherine airport, and how old Roger used to always go down the airport and wash the aeroplane for Dr Fenton. Dr Fenton was the flying doctor, he was the first plane in this country.

> Clyde (Doc) Fenton was one of the best known identities of the Northern Territory, pre and post war. During the war he was attached to Headquarters North Western Area for 'special duties', and gained a reputation for servicing outlying isolated Radar Units, showing great airmanship, skill, and adaptability to operate out of unmade strips and beaches.
>
> From 'Brief Resume of RAAF Service— Clyde Cornwall Fenton OBE', author unknown

He had a little Tiger Moth, and he come in about 1920 and he was still there when the Japs bombed Darwin and Katherine. Anyway, Don Jambarlirli and his father, old Roger, worked for old Fenton, and after work they went home to where all the other Aborigines were sleeping and camping out in the caves.

Old George Russell, he was a friend of my father, old Bill Harney, he told me when the Japanese plane came over Katherine there was not much of a town there, and the Japs saw the airstrip and they saw this round rock where the caves were, and they said, 'This must be a house, or a tarp over some supplies.' But it was a white rock where that old man Roger was living, and the Japanese said, 'Throw one in there!' and they dropped the bomb where these Aboriginal people were inside in the cave.

Well, old Roger come out to have a look, but the bomb ended on his head, poor bugger, and killed him. Old Roger had a little daughter and she got split open in the neck—a nasty cut around the head and everywhere, which bled, but it never killed her. She survived because she was well inside the cave with some of them others. That little girl is pretty old these days. Anyhow, it was only Roger got killed.

Chapter Six

COULD BE EQUAL

T hen after old Joe and Harry delivered the cattle to the
army at Manbulloo, we went on and walked past Katherine up to the Donkey Camp past the hospital there,
and that's when I saw old Bill Harney again, at the Donkey
Camp. That's up the river a bit where the old donkey men
used to have their donkeys. Old Bill had been working with
old Burt Drew on the donkey team, and before old Burt Drew
died, old Bill Harney said, 'Oh well, I'll give the donkey team
away,' and he come in and took a job with the Welfare, and
the Welfare had a depot up at the old Donkey Camp.

> . . . in 1939 E.W.P. Chinnery came from New Guinea to set
> up the Native Affairs Branch [a government organisation set
> up to administer Aborigines affairs] with a new deal for the
> Aborigines . . . V.J. White was second in charge as Chief Clerk,
> and the combined staff at that time was seven. At the time I
> was driving my own motor-truck for the Department of Public
> Works, and on being approached to join the Branch I sent in
> an application for the job. I was accepted, and in September
> 1940 I was made a Protector of Aborigines.
>
> From W.E. Harney, *Life Among The Aborigines*, Lansdowne Publishing, Sydney, 1995

He was looking after Aboriginal people like what the Aboriginal done for him in the first place when he came back from
overseas at the war, and old Bill Harney was boss man for the
Aborigine.

One day when I was there, just a kid, the army came
along and they asked to go around in the bush with old Bill,
and old Bill said, 'Oh yes, we'll take a gun.'

The army bloke reckons, 'Oh? What's that for? To shoot
more Aborigine in the bush?'

Old Bill said, 'Shoot Aborigine! I just got this gun to get a kangaroo. We'll cook it up in the bush, because I was taught from the Aborigine how we can cook it, and you can eat it.'

I followed them along, just listening to what I could hear, and they come across some wild old Aborigines who were still living wild in the bush amongst the hills around that Katherine area. Some had never seen a white man before, and some of the army blokes had never seen a blackfella either, and these Aborigines saw all these army men coming and they said, 'Oh look out! Some army coming, they might want to shoot us.'

Bill Harney could talk to the Aborigine with the finger— that's hand signals—and first he made a hand signal for 'white man'. Then he got his hand and waved his hand in his mouth. That means, 'We just come to talk, don't get fright.' Old Bill Harney first learned this finger talk around Bathurst Island, Melville Island, Groote Eylandt, and right through to Darwin and Mandorah. Then when he got down to the Wardaman country around Willeroo district he learned a lot of the finger talk from that country.

Anyway, the army blokes were all staring at old Bill doing the finger talk, and the old Aborigines started nodding their heads, and Bill Harney said to them, '*Yu kamap hiya en jidan dijlat en tok la im.*' That's English in a Kriol way and that means, 'You come up here, sit down this lot here, and talk with him.' Then everyone started to nod their head, and the army blokes went over close by and they all sat down together and had a yarn, and old Bill was explaining to the army blokes about the finger talk.

He said, 'To say "come with me" you gotta nod your head. For "fire" you fold your fists up and shake it real fast.'

Then these army blokes asked, 'What's the signal for a drink of water?' and old Bill showed them, waving his hand in his mouth like a fan.

Anyway they had a little billy and they used that to make a cup of bush tea from *yarlarr*, a low bush with a very scenty smell. It's medicine for your 'flu, for your asthma, and everything. But they didn't have any sugar, so they went and

COULD BE EQUAL 39

got some sugarbag then, that's the honey from the native bee. She makes a honeycomb like the European bee, but he is the native bee. He doesn't do any harm to anybody because he hasn't got a sting. He just minds his own business, and he goes around and picks up all these flowers off the tree and takes it back to his little nest and makes honey out of it. There is one lot of native bees makes the honey in the anthill—that looks a bit like treacle, black molasses, and we call that one *limwarrga*— the ground sugarbag. Another native bee makes the honey in a hole in the rock, and we call this one in the rock *yaramarrgu*. Another makes the honey in the hollow up the top of the tree, and that one is like the golden syrup. To get him out of the tree, you have to split the tree in half, then you just scoop the sugarbag out with your hand.

Anyway, the army went off to get some sugarbag from the tree, and these army blokes couldn't work out how these Aboriginal people could cut a tree. 'What with?' they said.

One of these boys picked up a little stone axe. He said, 'I cut it with this.'

This army bloke said, 'It's a bit blunt, isn't it?'

Well this boy spotted this sugarbag up in this tree and he chopped this tree down with this little stone axe. He made a little hole in the wood, and was poking all the honey with a little stick, and the honey's coming down onto a little piece of bark. It was unbelievable for the white man to see this, and he says, 'Now what do you do?'

The boy said, 'You take the sugarbag honey over to the waterhole and put water in this tin, and put all the honey into it, and get a certain grass and mash it all up to make it soft so you can suck it.'

He gave it to this Yankee American bloke and he start sucking it and he said, 'Well goddamn! This is very nice! This the way you live eh?'

The boys said, 'Yeah, this the way we live.'

'Could we take some of this home to the other persons?' and he took it back and gave it to the lieutenants, colonels and sergeant majors and provos and Christ knows what, and a lot of these old Yankee soldiers said, 'Goddamn, this is the way youse living. We only livin' on the biscuits and tinned beef. We didn't know the way youse were living. Is this the way you live all the time?'

The old boys said, 'Yeah, this is the way we live, like that now.'

The Yankee said, 'What do you use for beef?'

'We get kangaroo.'

'What with?'

'With a spear.'

'When it's running flat out?'

'Yeah.'

'Really! Well let's go out hunting,' the army said. Next thing this old kangaroo is racing across and this boy throws the spear and the kangaroo got the spear. And the old Yankee bloke looked and he said 'Goddamn! How did you get that? He's going pretty fast. I think he's goin' too fast for me for my eyesight. I don't think I could do that with a gun!' They raced across and sure enough the old kangaroo was down and they took it over under this tree, and this old boy picked up these firesticks and he started making a fire. He was rubbing away there and the old Yankee bloke looked and he gradually said, 'Goddamn! How could you make a fire just rolling that little firestick around?'

See, you can't just make a firestick out of anything, and old Bill was explaining to the Yankees: 'You hunt 'round and find a plum tree, get the dry limb off that and cut 'em in half and rub it together. They call this one *buda*.'

The Yanks were all watching there, looking, and this old boy just give couple of rubs with the sticks and it come on alight. 'Well! I'll be damned,' all the Yankees said, 'that's great! Never seen anything happen like this. Look at it, he's making a big fire with it. It's unbelievable!' And they cooked the kangaroo and, 'Oh, Jesus,' the army said, 'we'll have to get some of these Aborigine men and put them in the army,' and that's when they got a lot of the old boys, you know, and they joined the army, and they were in the army camps for a long time.

Up to and following the Japanese bombing of Darwin, which began on 19 February 1942, the non-Aboriginal population of the Northern Territory was evacuated to such places as Adelaide. Many Aboriginal children of mixed parentage, who lived in government institutions and missions, were also evacuated. That left approximately 100,000 soldiers and about 14,000 Aborigines living in the NT.

As the bombing of Darwin continued, a Japanese invasion was feared. All soldiers were occupied in military activities, and the army needed labourers. So the Native Affairs Branch and the army established labour camps along the North–South Road (Stuart Highway)—at places such as Mataranka, Larrimah, Manbulloo and Adelaide River—and enlisted Aborigines to work for them. Unlike on the cattle stations, the Aborigines who worked for the army were given proper food, sleeping quarters and pay, and by 1944 about 3000 Aborigines were employed by the forces. W.E. (Bill) Harney was full-time administering the 'natives' in these camps.

Jan Wositzky

And old Bill Harney was the boss man for the Aborigine in the army camps, and he used to explain to the Aborigine, 'As soon as the bell rings in the mornin' you gotta get up quick and get your boots on and race into the shower and get cleaned up. Whatever you want to do in the toilet, it gotta be a fast one. Then you gotta be lined up in the queue.' They lined up, and the army gave them Sao biscuits. But they wouldn't eat them because they was in the bush all their life and they had never seen these biscuits—just like the Yankees had never seen the sugarbag. Anyhow, gradually they learned to eat these biscuits and tinned beef, but as soon as they ate the tinned beef they started spewing. Then they explained to them to eat properly with a knife and fork. Well, the poor Aboriginal, as soon as the white man looked away he was dipping his finger in again, and as soon as the white man looked back he grabbed his knife and fork and sit down trying to cut this meat with the knife and fork.

Not too many Wardaman came to work for the army, only just three or four. They were just being a guide, and washing up dishes and things like that, and when they came back they told us the stories. 'Different style of way the white man go,' they said. 'You gotta wash your hands, you gotta brush your hair and you gotta wash your teeth, and you gotta wear clean clothes all the time, otherwise they tie you up and they put you in jail. You gotta have a clean shave. But we different,' that's what they reckoned.

Then some of the Aborigines that were in the army camp said they got well treated there because they got lots of food, and they was classed like any other European that was in the army camp. The army paid wages too. They used to dress them up in the army clothes, and they reckoned this was ideal, even if they was only just washing dishes and cleaning up around the army camps, and polishing up the colonel and lieutenant's shoes. They reckon it was great, see.

So the experience for the Aborigine from working in the army camps was that they got treated there like an equal with the white man. In the past on the cattle station they wasn't treated equal like the white man—they were just the Aborigine in the camp. They were working in the stock camp and they were classed as a good man, all right, but they weren't treated like the army did it. That's when they really started to solve the problem that started when the European did the wrong thing by firing a shot at the Aborigine in the first place, when the Aborigine moved into the army camp and found out that they could be equal.

Chapter Seven

FLOUR DISSOLVES THE FIGHT

Anyway, after we were out there at the Donkey Camp to have a yarn with Bill Harney, and all the Aboriginals out there showed the Yankees the bush food, we come back into Katherine town. Katherine was just a small place then. There was the old bakery where they used to bake the bread, and old Eric March had a Land Rover garage and he was using a Land Rover for a taxi. Katherine was just the police station, and in the wartime there was just C.J. Cox & Co., the old Katherine store.

That started off in 1926, but long before my time when the road was just an old Aboriginal pad, Katherine town was never there. She was set up to supply the goods to the many cattle properties on the western side, and they chopped a huge number of trees down in the country to build Katherine town. It was a bush timber town for a long while, but next the white ants came along eating the roofs off the buildings, and they said, 'Oh, might be we can build a stronger building that would be white ant proof.'

Then they saw Aborigines' spears landing on a rock and not breaking, so they headed across and said to the old Aborigines, 'I saw you throw the spears, it hit the rock and didn't break. What's the wood like? It must be a good strong wood, eh?'

The Aborigines said, 'Yeah. It's a very good strong wood.'

The bloke said, 'What about when you leave them laying in the ground, do the white ants eat them?'

'No, he doesn't eat them at all.'

'Well, can you take me out and show me what the tree looks like?' So the old Aborigines took him out to show him the tree and they tried to chop it down with the axe and they couldn't cut it. Then they went back and got a crosscut saw and the broad axe and they came out and chopped that tree down.

Well that new timber house lasted a while and then later on one bloke put up an angle-iron steel building that they used to call a 'Sydney Williams hut'. So everybody said, 'Oh, this is ideal because it's white ant proof,' and then everybody put up a steel building. But the roof of iron was cracking in the hot summer time, so they decided to knock the wall out and make a cool one from the termites' nest. They said, 'We've got enough Aborigines here to go out to get some termite nest in the bush and so build up our termite nest wall.' So they came out and picked up lots and lots of termite nest with the old wagonette and a lot of Aboriginals were crushing it up with the hammer and axe and wetting it and putting the sides of the house up, like a cement. 'It's nice and cool, it's not hot any more'—that's what the people said.

At the same time, this termite nest had a lot of moisture in it, and the hornet came along and started building nests and buzzing around people's heads, and they chased people out of their house. They said, 'This is no good, we must knock the termite wall down because there's too many hornets coming in.' They said, 'Surely to Christ we can make a brick house like they got down south.'

Then one bloke put a brick house up and then they started ordering the bricks down from Darwin. An old train used to come down once a fortnight. Then someone had an idea and he asked the old Aborigines, 'Do you know any good sand around here in this country?'

The old Aborigine said, 'Yes, I'll take you down and show you where the good sand is,' and he brought him all the way out to the King River, and there was the King River sand.

The whitefella said, 'Oh, this would be ideal sand to make bricks out of,' and they went back and set up a factory in Katherine to make lots of bricks to build Katherine town.

The 'Kath-Rhyne' (as it was often pronounced) ... was the name given to the Overland Telegraph Station built on the south bank of the Katherine River. Built by an expansionist South

Australian Government to strengthen its claim to the N.T., the
O.T. Line provided the reason for permanent European
settlement . . . and was opened on August 22, 1872 . . . On April
1st 1883, the Katherine telegraph station also became a post
office . . . By 1883, most of the original O.T. Line posts had
become termite tucker . . . The old O.T. station had gone the
same way.

From Mike Canavan, *The Katherine 1872–1917*, Katherine Historial Society, 1989

When we went into Katherine in the wartime, poor old
Bob Wood and them other policemen at the old police station
used to give us rations. Everything was given to you free.
They'd take your name, and give you flour, tea and sugar. I
think it was sort of the government support. And the drover
used to arrive and he always had a coupon for buying the food
and stuff, and the policeman used to cut the coupon in half
with the scissors. Then many drovers used to lead their packhorses right up to the veranda of the shop—some of them
always had a revolver on their hips and very long jingling
spurs—and they'd walk in, jingling away inside of the shop,
buying stuff, and walk out and pack their gear up into the pack
bag, and then they'd take off and tie their horses outside of the
pub and go in for a couple of beers.

There was a couple of pubs. One was old Bernard's
Hotel—that's where the Crossways pub is today—and another
one the Tim O'Shea Hotel—that's the Katherine Hotel now.
Anyway, the drovers were inside charging up and grogging on,
and there was a row of horses tied up outside, and if anyone
had a good-looking horse, some other bloke would run off
with his horse. If you got drunk and fall asleep and you had a
good-looking saddle on a horse, you'd wake up after and be
looking around where the saddle is, and it's gone! Of course
they put a policeman onto the bloke who pinched it, but he'd
be 20 or 30 mile away.

Anyway, all this sort of thing was carrying on, and Clyde
Fenton, the doctor in the aeroplane, he used to come over
from the original old airport to land outside the pub on the
dirt road. When he came along everyone'd say, 'Well, here's

Eagle Hawk Fenton coming, he's always flying around in the air,' and Clyde Fenton used to always walk in and have a drink with the ringers and drovers.

One day when Fenton was in there drinking there was a big brawl between old Fred Martin and old Wason Byers. Old Fred Martin was always nodding his head like a peregrine bird, so everyone called old Fred the Whispering Peregrine. Fred was always doing a lot of poddy-dodging—that's stealing cattle, all sorts, not just the poddy calves—and also thieving horses and stealing shoeing rasps, hammers and pincers—anything like that he used to thieve. They were all thieves in this country. All of them were second Ned Kellys, and one day in old Tim O'Shea's hotel old Fred Martin had a fight with Wason Byers.

And Wason Byers, he was worse than Hitler. He had no friends at all. Policeman were always frightened of him. Oh jeez, he was a big man. He'd do anything that bloke. He'd tie you up and leave you for a week. He had no mates. He didn't worry about anybody. We called him *Bullgup* because he liked *bullgupping* everyone—hammering everyone, with a strap or a stockwhip. In English he was called old 'Crooked-back Byers', because he had a bent back.

The first job he took as a head stockman was with Vesteys at Wave Hill, and of course the Aborigine didn't know him much, he was just the boss's man. But when he was yelling out and roaring, they knew he was a hard man. If it was a freezing cold morning and people couldn't get out of the bed, he used to drag the Aboriginal bloke out of the bed and swing them over his head and then throw them in the waterhole. When they come out of the waterhole he'd tell the boy to jump on the rooting horses, and of course they wouldn't get up on the rooting horses, and he'd burn their arse with the firestick. He was very cruel to the white man as well, oh Christ! If they did the wrong thing he'd grab them by the feet and tip them arse over head. When he paid you he'd only say, 'Here's ya cheque.' He wouldn't talk to you at all.

Anyway, this day Fred Martin heard that Wason Byers can fight, and he said to old Wason Byers, 'I heard that you could fight a bit,' he said, 'but I can too. I'm gunna challenge you to see who comes top.'

Byers said to old Fred, 'Oh you rubbish, you can't fight shit out of a paper.'

'All right,' Fred said, 'take your shirt off and let's get movin'.'

Old Fred took his shirt off and Wason Byers said, 'I won't take my shirt and hat off, you won't even knock the hat off my head.'

'Okay,' and they went into it. Everybody was looking, and everyone on Fred Martin's side was sayin', 'Oh, Fred won't last two punches because Byers is a very good fighter.' Well they got stuck into one another and Fred Martin cleaned Byers up and knocked him down quite a few times, and everybody was shouting and screaming and making Wason Byers more angry.

Then next, because Byers was really angry, he gets up and he picks up a 4-gallon pot-plant tin and crowned old Fred Martin and put him out, and everybody was clapping their hands and carrying on, and old Fred gets up and he starts crawling around. Old Fred always carried a revolver in the pommel of his saddle, and he raced out to his horse and pulled the revolver out and walked in again and started to fire a shot. Of course when Fred Martin fired his shot, Wason Byers fired one back, and Fred fired a shot again, and Fred Martin is on one end of the building and Wason Byers is on the other end of the building. They'd duck around, and every time they'd peep over they fired a shot, and the gunfight was carrying on there for a long while.

Of course old Tim O'Shea the publican, when he heard the shot, he raced away and hid in the corner. Clyde Fenton the pilot was there inside too, and he said, 'I think I can stop the fight,' and he worked it over in his mind. 'Only way to stop the fight,' he thought, 'is to buy some bags of flour, and come down in the plane and throw a few bags of flour onto the pub to make out it's like a bomb. That way they'll think it's the Japs and stop fighting.'

So he raced around to C.J. Cox & Co. and he picked up four or five bags of flour, and raced across and put them in his Tiger Moth, and he started his little plane up and he took off. When he came back, the fighting was still carrying on with the revolvers, with old Byers down one end of the bar and old Fred Martin up the other, and next thing Clyde Fenton dropped a bag of flour through the roof of the pub, and a big cloud of smoke went up in the air, and they said, 'Look out! The Japs coming! The Japs coming and throwin' the bomb!'

And Clyde come back down and dive-bombed them again. He'd go up in the air and he'd come down nose first— 'rrrrrrrrr'—and was throwing out these bags of flour and, oh Jesus, you couldn't see the pub for flour because flour after flour was coming down, yeah, oh Jesus! Anyway, Clyde Fenton come down again and he threw one bag of flour on top of roof and a big cloud of flour poured up like a big cloud of smoke, and everybody said, 'This is the army coming all right, the Japs!' They thought the atom bomb was coming. Old Fred Martin raced back and he jumped on his horse and away he galloped. Everybody was all hidden away. Everybody's horses had run away, and everyone was walking around on foot looking for their horses.

And that had worked for Clyde Fenton, it dissolved the fight. It was great of him, and old Fenton went back to the airport. About a couple a hours after, he came back and old Tim O'Shea's sitting down there with a big grin on his mouth and he saw Clyde Fenton. 'Well, Clyde,' he said—he was an old shamrock one, you know, from the green island, an Irishman, they used to call him 'Mullaka Cup o' Tea', old man cup of tea—and he said, 'Well Clyde, to thank you I'll give you a bottle o' rum, but you can have a drink with me first.'

Clyde said, 'What's that for, Tim?'

He said, 'You did that very good turn, because otherwise the house would'a had a lotta holes, and probably I would'a got shot. You did a good job to frighten 'em with the bags of flour. What made you think that idea to get the flour?'

'Well,' he said, 'I just worked up in me mind because I

had the plane outside, and that's when I went over and bought the flour and came down and dive-bombed the top of your hotel.' Anyway, they shook hands and had a drink together. And old Fred Martin and Byers were nowhere to be seen. They were off poddy-dodging somewhere in the country again.

Chapter Eight

PODDY-DODGERS

Before the war and all through the war, old Fred Martin and many other blokes, like the old drover Mick Cussens, and old Fordham who had a place over at Larrimah, and Dick Scobie who had a place called Hidden Valley, they were all over the country, poddy-dodging all the cattle, because they could sell them to the army. The army meatworks was over at the back of Manbulloo and another bloke, Noel Healey, had a small abattoir on the road at Dunmarra near Hidden Valley, and he was getting his meat from the poddy-dodgers. They were all in for a cut, thieving cattle off one another and everyone else for these abattoirs. One big bullock was worth about £2. With that you could buy three gaberdine trousers, six shirts, one boots, sombrero hat, leather chaps, and a belt. If they stole and sold twenty bullocks that was £40, and they were rich! But they were cutting one another's throat. Old Fordham was a second Ned Kelly, and he didn't care who he stole from. Mick Cussens was trying to rob old Scobie, and he was trying to rob old Fordham, and old Fordham was robbing old Mick Cussens.

One time old Mick Cussens came along with fifty horses he stole from Camooweal, and he had to get rid of these horses before the cops got him. Now Mick Cussens was a wonderful drover, the greatest drover I ever seen. He was taking cattle for Vesteys from 1930, and wherever he took the cattle he always learnt a lot of the Aboriginal songs. 'Wirwarra Mick' they used to call him, and as soon as he got drunk he always sang that song:

Warri warn gunya
Warri warn gunya
Gurn-gurn ali
Warn barnali
Warri warn gunya

I heard him in the bar one day and I said, 'Jeez! God! This old man knows this song!' I was surprised that he sang it. That song means you are worrying about your country, and you like to dance for your country. '*Warri warn gunya*' means that he left his country droving bullocks with the drover. That's not a Dreaming song, that's a *junba* song, a fun song. Anyway, Mick was singing in the bar and everyone yarded him up: 'Go on, Mick, ya doin' a good job!' And he continued singing away. Old Mick, ah Jesus, he was a wonderful man, and he told me lots of stories too, about all these Ned Kellys in the country who all used to pinch the horses and cattle.

Anyway, this time he was coming across past Daly Waters with these horses and he stopped at Larrimah Station with old Fordham. Fordham always wore a hat with a big brim right over his nose, and he was always moving the hat, all around his head. He'd be talking to you, and moving it forwards, then over to the right, then shoving the hat backwards, then over to the left. That was his style, and old Fordham was talking to Mick Cussens and that night they got a couple of cases of rum and they really got old Mick drunk as a monkey. Mick Cussens was drunk for three or four days, and while he was drunk old Fordham hid these horses away in the scrub. When Mick come to he said, 'Oh well, I been drunk here nearly a week. I better go and look for my horses.'

Old Fordham said, 'I haven't seen sight of your horses here. But I got a couple of horses there, we'll jump on one each and we can go out and look for 'em.'

Mick Cussens said, 'Okay,' and they saddled up and went out looking for these horses.

But Fordham didn't take him to the place where he hid those horses. Fordham took these horses through the strainer fence and right around through Warlock Ponds and come in behind his place. 'Gawd,' old Fordham says, 'how could those horses get away?' Mick Cussens was worrying, and old Fordham said, 'Some crook must be 'round this area.' Poor Mick Cussens had no horses to go anywhere, and Fordham reckons, 'You got money to buy a couple of horses off me? You could go down to Hidden Valley and try and get some horses off Scobie.'

Mick Cussens reckons, 'Oh well, I'll give you £5 for one horse,' and Fordham gave him this one horse and Mick was riding back to Hidden Valley to where old Dick Scobie lived. Not so long ago they grew a big marijuana plantation there, because Hidden Valley was always a good place to hide away, and when old Dick Scobie had it he never went to sleep—he was up all night raiding the country for other men's cattle. He always had a ten-gallon hat on his head, with a little dash in the front and a high crown, and a stockwhip over his shoulder, and a big long spur, and he was a funny, jokeable bloke.

Anyway, it was a fair way from Larrimah Station up to Hidden Valley, and Mick Cussens ran out of tucker on the road, and he was trying to get some little billabong crabs to have a feed. When he got down to Hidden Valley, Mick was telling Scobie he was hungry as buggery. He said, 'You have to get a thousand of them before you could get a feed, it's all shell. I nearly eat the whole shell, but I was worrying about these horses of mine.'

Old Scobie told him nobody came through with the horses. 'The horses never turned up at all,' he said. 'You sure that Fordham never hid those horses of yours?'

Mick Cussens reckons, 'Oh jeez, that might be it too! He might have hid them away because we was drunk for a week. Well,' he said, 'I must go back and see old Fordham.'

Dick Scobie give him another two or four horses to get back, and a bit of tucker, and he rode back and seen old Fordham and Fordham said, 'Did you chase up where those horses went to?'

Mick Cussens said, 'Something unusual here, these horses must be still in the country.'

Fordham says, 'I reckon you can go through as many pad-docks as you like. You can go through the whole lot. You can take the young fella with you. Search one paddock, another paddock, another paddock, another paddock.'

Well, old Mick went through three or four paddocks and he couldn't find any of them. Fordham had them about 50 mile out to Yarangon Plain. Mick Cussens came back and he told old Fordham, 'I can't do nothing. How can I shift all my gear, all my packs? I only got one packhorse off old Scobie to travel back again. I have to buy some more horses. You got any more horses for sale?'

Fordham said, 'I got no more horses to sell you, Mick.'

Then another old poddy-dodger, old Jack Blackman, come along. He was a Wardaman and he was taken away in about 1920 because he was a half-caste. He was taught at school, and he didn't worry about cattle much—he just used to steal horses and skin-graft and re-brand them. Anyway, Jack Blackman come along, said g'day to Mick, and Mick told him about the horses he lost, and Mick said that he wanted to go over to see his friend old McNamara over at Lissadell, right over in the west, because he might have some horses.

Jack Blackman always talked with his head down, and he said, 'That's very dry country, Mick. There not much water at any bore along the Murranji stock road. You'll perish through that way.'

Mick reckons, 'I'll get through.'

Then Jack said, 'There's one bore only every 30 mile.' That's about every 50 kilometres.

But Mick reckons, 'Well, I got to go and see if I can get some horses.'

Jack said, 'What about a camel instead of the horse out in the dry country?' And Mick looked at him.

'You could do it with a camel team,' said Jack. 'They can carry two forty-four drums full of water.'

'Oh yeah?' old Mick Cussens reckons. 'But where could I get some?'

'I know where I could get some.'

'Whereabouts?'

'Some over at Inverway, all the Afghans over there. Big heap of camels. I could go over and get some for you, and I'll hide 'em away in Hidden Valley for you.'

Mick said, 'Yeah?'

Jack said, 'But you're gunna have to give me some money.'

Mick Cussens said, 'No worries, I'll give you some money,' and old Jack Blackman went across to Inverway to get some camels.

Now first these camels come into the country with the old Afghans from overseas, and they used them for carting the stores over the desert. At first the old Aboriginal people thought the camel was a devil, like they did when they first saw the horse, only this one with the big hump on the back. One old Aboriginal man, old Jabiru, was telling me he was walking home to VRD with his wife and they see a camel. They'd never seen a camel before and they reckoned, 'Oh, Jesus! Big ghost coming!' and they took off up this tree yelling and trying to get this old camel to go away, and the camel was not taking much notice at all—just sitting and just looking at them. Jabiru said the old camel was just sitting back eating grass and looking at them, and they was there nearly half the night. Then early in the morning they jumped down from the tree and took off and told these other blokes that they had seen the great big devil over there: 'Oh, great big tall one with a big hump on his back.'

The manager Alf Martin said, 'That's a camel. He won't hurt you because they a very tame animal.'

Jabiru said, 'We're going to go over and kill this big devil we seen.'

'It's not a devil at all,' he said, 'it's a camel. I'll go over and get it if you want it. You watch me.' Anyway, old Alf Martin goes over near the camel and the old dang camel was just fooling around, and old Jabiru is watching him, and after that they knew it was a camel, and he was good for travelling that country with no water on it.

Anyway, old Jack Blackman goes over to Inverway to get the camels from the old Afghans, and he was talking to old

Sarlie Mohammed. Old Sarlie used to carry the stores from Wyndham to all the stations, and he couldn't talk much English, and he was a bugger for playing dice with the Aborigines. He had a wife from the Gurindji tribe, and his face was totally different to the Aboriginal of this country. He was a Muslim I think, and Jack Blackman says to old Mohammed, 'I'll book up some tucker and when our droving season starts I'll pay you for what I owe you.'

'All right,' Sarlie Mohammed reckons.

Jack said, 'By jeez old Sarlie, you got some nice camels over there.'

'Yeah,' he said. 'I go down and pick up all the stores from the jetty at Wyndham and bring all my tucker up here.' He had about a hundred camels, old Sarlie Mohammed did. Anyway, blow me, old Jack Blackman stole twenty camels off him and he's heading across with them camels. He didn't quite call into Wave Hill; he missed Montejinni; he come across to Murranji and back to Hidden Valley.

Old Scobie spotted him coming across with these camels and said, 'Gawd strike me dead! I seen some blokes that steal horses and cattle, but I haven't seen a bloke who can steal a camel!'

Jack Blackman was riding up there and he says, 'I got some nice camels here.'

Scobie reckons, 'Yeah, what're you gunna do with the camels?'

Jack Blackman says, 'You know what? On these stock roads there's one bore only every 30 mile. You gotta go dry-camping two or three nights before you can get to that bore. I was talking to old Mick Cussens and Mick Cussens wants camels to take a 44 gallon drum of water for him.' That's about 200 litres. And old Scobie reckons, 'That's quite a good idea.'

Anyhow, Mick Cussens come along, and he said, 'Did you get those camels for me?'

'Yeah.'

'Oh well,' he said, 'I'll give you £5 a head for them. You've done a very good turn for me going down and getting 'em off the old Afghans.'

Then old Mick Cussens took off back east over to Camooweal side with this big heap of camels.

In the mean time, old Sarlie Mohammed was mustering the camels up to get a big load of rations from Wyndham jetty and he was short of about twenty camels, and Sarlie Mohammed was going really mad about these camels. 'I think it's that bloke who come across here. He's a bit of a thieving bloke and he's been taking stolen horses from many stations. Old Jack Blackman!' he said. 'He's the bloke to see. I wonder which way he was heading?' Some of the old wild Aboriginal people living in the hills spotted the camels when old Jack Blackman come through and they went back and reported that Jack Blackman was heading across with all these camels to Hidden Valley, and they got on to the policeman, old Jack Mahoney, at Larrimah about Jack Blackman stealing this big heap of camels.

Anyway, Mick Cussens is going through to Camooweal with the camels and he heard about the big Afghan store out on the Rankin Plain, and he went out there and all the Afghans spotted all these camels and said, 'Gawd, I like those old camels. Where did you get them from? No Australian people have any of 'em camels, only the Afghan have that many. Do you speak any words for them camels?'

Mick Cussens said, 'How the hell you make 'em go lay down?'

They told him the Afghan word for 'lay down' and one old camel lays down and old Mick Cussens put a drum of water on his side and Mick tried to yank the old camel up. The old camel wasn't taking any notice—he just lay down there—and next thing old Mick Cussens gets behind him with a whip and tries to make the old camel get up. The Afghans are watching and they're getting upset, and they tell Mick the Afghan word for 'get up', and the camels get up and Mick keeps going.

Then when they're pulling up for lunch old Mick Cussens was trying to make this old camel lay down so he can take his tucker off—his lunch was up the top, see—and the old camel wouldn't take notice. Mick couldn't remember the Afghan word, and he said, 'Oh blow this old camel, I'm gunna shoot the lot,' and he got out his old .44 and shot all the camels he had. And that's what Mick Cussens done with all the camels. Oh Christ!

Anyway, old Mick Cussens got some more horses and he went down to Newcastle Waters to see his uncle and on the way he was selling these horses for a bottle of rum. An old Afghan bloke had a stall with a gallon licence and Mick sold him five horses for five bottles of rum, and he kept on going and he finished up around Halls Creek area and he went down and seen old McNamara who was at Lissadell—that was his friend. They were having a yarn and McNamara said, 'Well Mick, I'll give you droving this year. You can take a load of cattle to Queensland.'

Mick said, 'I haven't got any horses.'

McNamara said to him, 'What happened to the horses?'

'I was broke along the road. I had to sell those horses for a bottle of rum. One horse was for a bottle of rum.'

Old McNamara looked at him, he said, 'Gawd Christ! You wouldn't do that would you? Why did you do that? You make your money with those horses to do the droving. You don't have to sell the horses for a bottle of rum.'

'Well,' he said, 'I did.'

Old McNamara said, 'Look, I'll give you some horses and you can start off taking this mob of cattle back to Queensland.'

'All right,' old Mick Cussens said, and he come across with the cattle. He had a team of black boys with him, and when he got to Auvergne old Slippery Prendergast was in front of him with another thousand head. When they got to Newcastle Waters, old Mick Cussens had his cattle on one end of the plain, and Slippery had his mob of cattle on the other end of the plain. They called him Slippery because he always greased his saddle to make it look shiny, and then he always had slippery strides see, and that night old Slippery and old Mick Cussens went down the bar and had a few rums and come back to these cattle, and what happened, some drunk fell over on the canteen and the mob of cattle rushed and all the Auvergne cattle and the Lissadell cattle were mixed up.

The next thing, old Mick Cussens and old Slippery were

having a row. They were all tanked up with the rum and shout-ing, 'We got two thousand head in the mob now and we gotta start drafting! We haven't got a camp horse each! What we gunna do?'

Well, they mainly had a mob of blacks with them in those times because they was cheap to work, and these blacks go down and start drafting all the cattle. At the same time, another drover was bringing a lot of old Beetaloo cattle in to the water on this plain, and these Beetaloo cattle are getting boxed up with the Auvergne and Lissadell cattle. The mob is getting bigger and bigger and bigger and bigger and bigger and bigger and bigger. Old Mick Cussens looked over. 'Gawd,' he said, 'look at the mob. There's not a thousand head at all, they look like about three or four thousand.'

Slippery said, 'Oh, we go down and have a look.' What happened, these three or four blackfellas watching the cattle wasn't taking much notice—just letting all these other Beetaloo cattle come in and getting boxed up with Mick and Slippery's cattle—and old Mick Cussens got stuck into two or three of these blacks, and gave them a hiding with a whip.

Next morning old Mick goes out to begin drafting again, and he's calling out to these three boys and these three boys weren't there at all. They took off in the night after Mick whipped them, and Mick Cussens was saying, 'Where is those black mongrels? They're not there,' and sure enough they was gone. Then Mick Cussens was desperate. He said, 'I'm gunna give another blackfella a hiding! God-almighty, what they do to me! I gotta suffer it now! I started off with a thousand head, now I got about three or four thousand on my hands.' Then he said, 'Anyway, we'll let any cow with a calf go, and just hang on to any big stuff.'

Then when they was rounding the cattle up, they were nearly all Beetaloo cattle, and Mick Cussens was disappointed. 'Gawd! Where's all Lissadell cattle? They're all gone and we only got Beetaloo mob now. God-almighty!' he said, and it took them about nearly a week to muster the cattle because they was in lancewood scrub and bullwaddy scrub right through. Mick ended up getting about eight hundred out of it, and he lost two hundred—he was pleased to get something of that anyway—and then he got them down to Dajarra and he said, 'I'll never do droving again on that stock road. Every time I come past Newcastle Waters there's always a big mob of cattle in the road, and you get on the scoot and all the cattle get boxed up. It's no good.'

Then old Slippery Prendergast said, 'Well, you gotta be more careful and look after your stock the proper way, not just bashing the men up and then letting 'em get away from you. It's no good.'

Anyway, old Mick Cussens was worrying about these lost two hundred head of old McNamara's cattle, and he got on the rum and the metho and essence of lemon. He really got on it, and he went off his head and he started taking fits, and he took off bush on foot. He was in the horrors and no one could find him—they thought he drowned or something—then after three or four days the police tracker found old Mick Cussens sitting in one of these gidgee trees, talking to himself, with no shirt on, no boots—he only had strides on. They sneaked over to him very close and sung out to him, 'Mick,' but he wouldn't listen to them. He was off his head altogether. They just got close to him and grabbed him and they took old Mick Cussens back to Mt Isa and they put him in a truck and took him to the lunatic asylum. I don't know where that place is, but he was there for about nearly four or five years and he come back good again, normal.

Anyway, in the meantime, old Fordham, who stole the horses of Mick Cussens, was always away thieving cattle, off Montejinni, VRD, Roper Valley area and Hodgson Downs area and Elsey area and all that. And Fordham come back with all these cattle, and he sold them to Noel Healey, who had a butcher shop over at Dunmarra. All the poddy-dodgers around that district, Scobie and Mick Cussens and Fordham, all used to sell a helluva lot of their cattle to Noel Healey.

Chapter Nine

A PILE OF BONES

N oel Healey had a bit of a butcher and a slaughtering yard at Dunmarra, and old Healey used to always say, 'Bring those cattle over and we'll go through 'em,' and he used to feed a lot of those Yank army blokes making the bitumen road from Darwin to Mt Isa and Alice Springs.

> It is common belief that during World War Two the United States military bituminised the North–South Road, now known as the Stuart Highway—but the story is untrue. Using US equipment, the bitumen was laid by the roads departments of various Australian state governments, each state taking a different section of the road, and completing the job in double-quick time. However, the mythology that only the Americans could have got it done so quickly still persists.
> Information from *Main Roads* magazine, September 1946

Anyway, a fella called Jack Liddell used to work for Noel Healey, and when Jack was the manager at Willeroo in about 1950, he was telling me about Noel Healey. Close to Dunmarra, where Healey had his butcher shop, was Hidden Valley, where old Scobie had his place, and one day Noel Healey says to old Scobie, 'Could you bring me some scrub bullocks?'

Scobie says, 'Oh, yeah, I could bring you some nice beautiful scrub bullocks.'

'All right.'

Well Scobie goes out over around Montejinni area and he tracked about three hundred or four hundred VRD cattle and he brings them over and he sells them to Noel Healey. When Noel Healey was killing them and he had the last two bullocks in the yard, the manager from VRD, old Alf Martin, arrived. He was just coming back from his holiday, and he pulls up there and he walks over to the yard to have a look. Luckily Noel Healey spotted him and he took the ear mark and the brand off the hide and threw it away. Old Alf walks over and he spoke to Noel Healey. He said, 'By jeez, that's a beautiful bullock, eh? Where did you get all these bullocks from?'

'Oh,' he said, 'off Scobie. He got some nice cattle in that area.'

'Oh,' he said, 'would be too, eh.' But Alf Martin didn't know it was all VRD cattle, and he just went home to VRD.

Anyway, when Noel Healey used to kill a killer—that's a bullock we cut up for our own meat—he used to throw a helluva lot of bones away on a pile about 20 mile out the back of the butcher shop. Well, there used to be a helluva lot of wild blacks around that area—around Daly Waters side and Dunmarra and Newcastle Waters, everywhere around there— and the blacks used to always wait till Noel Healey chucked all his bones away at the dump, and make a dive and eat the bones up.

And Noel Healey saw that the bones were disappearing and he said, 'A lot of dingoes must be 'round this area.'

Well, the manager from Newcastle Waters come along, and he says to Noel Healey, 'A lot of me calves were taken away, eaten by the dingo.'

'Yeah, I noticed that,' Noel Healey said, 'because every time I take a carcass down to the dump the bones all disappear.'

Anyway, the manager said, 'Well, I'll help you along, we'll get some strychnine and put some strychnine in the bones, and we might collect a few dingoes.'

See, in that time the cattle stations used to employ a dogger in this country to clean all the dingoes out because the dingo was killing all the calves. The dogger used to split some meat in half and put a little bit of strychnine along the groove, and when the dog come along and ate it they'd be getting giddy, then they get druggy, and they go to sleep and die. Then the dogger took a piece of his ears and tail and stringed them up on a wire, and then the policeman used to stand up with his cheque and count them, all ready to pay a pound a head. Nowadays they're flying around up in the air just pouring out lots of meat from the airplane, but what's happening there is the first one to come along is the goannas and lizards, and they're the first ones to go before the dogs.

So old Noel Healey poisoned a lot of these bones with strychnine, and the Aborigine was hidden there in the scrub just waiting, and as soon as Noel Healey unloaded the bones at the dump and went back, the Aborigines just raced across and picked up all these bones to cook them. They didn't realise he had put strychnine in them, and the next thing all these wild Aboriginal people were dying because they ate the strychnine. Aboriginal people were dying everywhere in the bullwaddy scrub, lying under where the branches bend over and the leaves touch the ground.

Old Noel Healey didn't mean to poison the blacks at all, he was after the dingoes, and then later the manager from Newcastle Waters come along and says to Noel Healey, 'What about we go out and look see if we got any dingoes,' and they jumps on a horse each and away they went. When they got 20 mile out of Dunmarra they could smell something, and they went over to have a look. And when they got down there, there were nearly forty or fifty blacks, dead in the scrub. 'Goddamn!' old Noel Healey says to this manager. 'How come all these blackfellas died? Somebody shot 'em? Must have been Scobie, he must've got into 'em, eh?' They were Mudbra blacks.

They looked around and they couldn't find any bullet marks, but they could see all these bones. 'Gawd,' old Healey said, 'you know what we done? I tell you what happened. When we poisoned all those bones, a lot of these old blacks come along and started getting all these bones and that's what they're dying of.'

'Oh,' the manager said, 'that could be it too. I think that's why all my cattle are going off from Newcastle Waters, they're getting speared by wild Aboriginal people.' Anyway, they go back and report it to the policeman, old Jack Mahoney at Daly

Waters, and old Jack has a look, and sure enough there was a lot of dead wild Aboriginal people.

In those times, if any whites got speared, the copper would be on the ball, but if Aboriginal people got shot or poisoned they just used to let it go. 'That's all right,' they used to say, 'just leave it. Dingo can eat him.'

And Jack Mahoney the policeman and old Noel Healey went back and Noel said, 'We better not throw any of this strychnine over at the dump again, eh? We could chuck the bones at the dump again but not with the strychnine.'

Anyway, Noel Healey carried on and one day some Aboriginal people from Newcastle Waters rode up to him and said, 'Mullaka,'—*Mullaka* means old fella, boss—they said, 'them wild blackfella they're after you because you poisoned a lot of boys in the bush.'

Noel Healey said, 'I didn't poison any boys, I was only poisoning for dingo.'

'Well,' they said, 'I heard 'em talking about it. They're gunna come 'round and spear you.'

'Spear me?'

'Yeah, they're gonna spear you, just get high on opium and keep yourself covered.'

Well the wild blackfellas were sneaking up on him and trying to spear him, and old Noel used to lock himself up in Dunmarra and they couldn't get him. He always had a firearm and they were frightened of him, and couldn't get close with a spear. Noel Healey was a bit frightened too and he said, 'I better sell the place up before they kill me,' and he advertised and let somebody else take over, and he closed his butcher shop, and the next thing Noel Healey just took off. All these wild Aboriginal people frightened him, and that was the end of old Noel Healey at Dunmarra.

Well old Noel Healey goes over to old Jack Mahoney at Daly Waters and he said, 'Those wild Aboriginal people chased me out of that district, what you gunna do about it?'

Jack Mahoney says, 'Well, we can't go out exploring and lookin' for all them Aboriginal people because they're all hid away in the bullwaddy and lancewood scrub. We can't see 'em till we come right on 'em and then we're likely to get a spear right through the ribs.'

Then Noel Healey reckoned to Jack Mahoney, 'What about you get a few police black-trackers to coax a lot of these old Aboriginal people to come in from the bush and be like the white man?'

Jack Mahoney says, 'Oh yeah, we'll try.'

They talked to this old Aboriginal police tracker and the tracker reckoned, 'I'm a police tracker but they might reckon I'm like a white man. If I go against 'em I'm likely to get a spear right through me too.' And this tracker said, 'They sing that rifle you know, so a bullet can't go off.'

Noel Healey said, 'Yeah?'

And Jack Mahoney said, 'Yeah, that's right, because old Tas Fitzer the other policeman was telling me.'

'That's right, they sing all right,' the tracker boy said. 'We better not interfere. They're likely to come back themselves and live amongst the white man's tribe later on, eh?'

The next thing, old Tim O'Shea from the hotel at Katherine comes along—Jack Mahoney was married to old Tim O'Shea's daughter—and he said, 'Look, Jack, I'll tell you what, only way to control the blacks is to give this tracker Jackie some packhorses and give him a few bags of flour and tea and treacle, and a few tins of meat, and he can go into the bush and coax the blacks in that way.'

Jack Mahoney said, 'Oh that's not a bad idea,' and that's what they did.

Chapter Ten

'BRING 'EM IN'

Old Jackie the tracker was Wardaman from Willeroo, and Jackie was my grandfa in the Aboriginal way— he was related to my Aboriginal father, Joe Jomornji. He had old Maggie for his wife—that was my old granny— and Jack Mahoney was talking to Jackie the tracker: 'Youse been in here workin', and I want you to bring all these wild blacks in here to be calm, to tame down, and they can work for me and the army all along this road. Tell 'em that you got food here, and that you been workin' in here, and explain to 'em that they can all come down. We can't shoot with anything, you know. Tell 'em everything will come real good. Go out there and bring 'em in.'

The idea was for Jackie to go on his own, because sometimes when the Aborigine took the white man with him into the bush it would backfire, because the old Aborigine would think the European was going out to shoot them. Anyway, old Jackie reckoned, 'All right, I'll go out and have a look 'round,' and old Jackie and his wife Maggie went out bush to bring in the blacks for Jack Mahoney.

A lot of these old wild blackfellas were living around the limestone caves, in the wattles and springs behind the fan palm country, and old Jackie went out and he says to these boys, 'The policeman sent me out here to talk to you mob, to tell you to go in and talk to the white man.' The wild old blackfellas were all sitting up looking at Jackie on the horse. Old Jackie said, 'Well, come in and be like a white man.' A lot of these real wild blackfellas reckoned he was only just kidding them, and old Jackie said, 'I wanna try and talk to you. Here look, I'll give you flour and sugar. You taste this bread from the white man's flour.'

Well they wouldn't touch that flour at all because they thought there might be strychnine in the flour, so old Jackie had a taste first and proved that there was no poison in it. The old blackfellas were looking at this flour, and some of them picked it up and were licking it with their mouths, testing it, and a lot of them reckoned, 'Oh, that's white paint,' and the next thing they used one bag of flour to paint themselves for a corroboree.

Old Jackie said, 'That's tucker. It's not paint for any corroboree. It's just flour. This is the way you mob do it,' he said, 'look.' And he had old Maggie start cooking up a big damper and johnnycakes and she gave them all a try.

They ate this damper and the johnnycakes and all the old wild blackfellas reckoned, 'By jeez, that was all right. They taste good. We'll eat all this now.'

Jackie said, 'Oh well, we gotta come 'round one day and pick you mob up and take you away, and some of the blokes from Elsey Station will take you to Mataranka to work on the station, and for the army.' (There was only an army camp around at Mataranka, there wasn't much at all, only a bit of a shop was there.)

Anyhow, they were all eating up, and old Jackie gradually come back to Daly Waters to tell old Jack Mahoney. He said, 'Well, I had a yarn to 'em but it took 'em a while before they got used to the flour and sugar and stuff.'

Jack Mahoney says to him, 'You go back and talk to 'em properly. Tell 'em all to come up this way.'

Jackie said, 'All right.'

Anyway, they went out and picked up all these old wild blackfellas and got them in to Daly Waters, and old Jack Mahoney was there and he explained to them, 'You be like a white man, like us mob. We can't shoot you or anything like that. Shooting days are over long ago. You gotta become like us, we all the same, only the colour's different. Black and white and yellow, they're nothing—only the colour's different. You gotta come up like us mob, talk sense and everything, English.'

They were giving them tobacco and they tasted it there,

all sitting around, all looking. They thought they were going to get poisoned, they wasn't too sure yet. And Jack Mahoney said, 'We go over and sit under the tree and I can explain English,' and he used to explain English to them.

After a while they reckoned, 'Oh, that's great,' and everybody went out in the bush again to bring some more in, and that way they brought the whole lot in from the bush.

Anyhow, gradually Jack Mahoney was asking Jackie, 'How do you mob live in the bush?'

Old Jackie started explaining, 'Oh, just a bit of yam, bit of goanna, bit of bush banana and then sugarbag, and a bit of porcupine, kangaroos, or emus now and again, and mussels and crab and all that.'

Some of the old Aboriginal blackfellas were nodding their heads and looking at Jack Mahoney and he reckons, 'God! If that's the way they live it must've been pretty hard, depressing to live like the Aboriginal people!'

And Jack Mahoney spotted this old girl carrying a *lijarri* full of seeds, and he and old Mrs Mahoney went over and asked everybody what it was. This old Aboriginal woman was just looking at them, and Maggie said, 'In the Aboriginal word they call it *mangurlu*—just like flour. It's a seed off the grass, and they crush it up with a flat stone. Bush seeds.' Then this old lady showed them how to cook it—to crush it all up on a big flat stone to make it a real fine powder similar to a flour, and get a cupful of water and wet it and make it like a damper, all round, and make a big fire, get all coals there and spread out all the ashes of the fire, and put the damper in these ashes and cover it all up, and leave it for an hour or so, and pull it out.

It's about four inches wide and a foot long, and it comes up not quite like flour—it's a bit heavy but it tastes very good, like crushing up a spud more or less. And Jack Mahoney and Mrs Mahoney reckons, 'Oh, jeez, that's a good flavour that.' Jack Mahoney and Mrs. Mahoney couldn't believe it. They said, 'This is a different way from the bags of flour. It looks a bit like the flour, but it doesn't rise, it's just a flat damper. But he fill you up. It's great.'

Well Jack Mahoney took a helluva lot of blacks back to Daly Waters where he had the police station there, and he was giving them flour and a lot of them was working for him. He went with the buggy down around Elsey area tracking a lot of them in the bush, and he brought them over to the European side and had them working for the army at Mataranka.

But when the war finished up and the army gradually disappeared and went away, they just left the Aborigine to operate in the pastoral area again. They still weren't treated as a good working man. None of them was on a wage, just working for shoes and a bit of food and a shirt and trousers. That's the way they were treated, that was part of their life, see. But they wasn't worrying about any money. They were back eating amongst themselves on the woodheap. That's the way they were brought up in the bush.

PART THREE

BOY TO MAN (1945–55)

Chapter Eleven

BLACK PLUM AND CHARCOAL

After the war was finished my dad, old Bill Harney, was still a Welfare man and he used to make a lot of visits right down to Wave Hill and VRD, and I used to see him talking to all the people there and writing on the paper.

REPORT ON PATROL WESTERN STATIONS

To:
Director
Native Affairs Branch
Sir,
On the 11th May acting under instructions from the branch, I proceeded to inspect the Western stations.

Natives and Welfare

I encountered and inspected over 700 natives on this patrol and of that number 307 are working on the stations as stockmen, yardbuilders, teamsters, domestics, assistant mechanics, butchers, truck drivers, etc.

The hours of this work is from daylight till late at night for every day of the week and the only holiday is when they are on walkabout, which in wartime very rarely occurs.

As usual with all these places a native is only looked upon as a labour unit, the health of the people only looked at, not from the human point of view, but because sickness causes a lowering of the labour unit, just as a horse with a sore back must be treated, because it cannot be worked efficiently otherwise. Thus a good stockman with ailing eyesight is looked after, but should this happen to the aged and infirm this is not the case.

Housing

In all cases with a few exceptions the housing conditions of these natives and their dependants is deplorable, any houses built in their own time after work. The materials they get for this is wood gathered in odd sorts of ways such as off the woodheap, or with the help of some sympathetic truck driver, or cast-off iron and petrol tins flattened out and nailed on with nails from packing cases. Believe me it is indeed pathetic to see these people trying to build a nice place while all the time the Managers, police, and all, join in with the everlasting cry of 'If you build houses for them they won't live in them.'

Imagine such conditions as these: The natives working all day, every day, no wages just bread and beef with tea and sugar, his wife if she is young is worked too, children also work if old enough. He is just told to do things and too frightened to disobey beause there is nowhere to go. Often old natives told me of their treatment and their desires but it was with lowered voice as though the trees had ears and the arm of the boss was long.

What is urgently required is correct supervision of natives on stations, or failing that, wages to be paid to all employees with good houses provided and their dependants gathered to suitable reserves and their welfare assured.

In these places all young native women and girls could be protected, not as today where the native women are regarded as part of the wages paid to keep men on the stations. It is an old saying in the bush that native women can retain their virtue only by having the speed of Costle (the sprinter) and the endurance of Nurmi (the long distance runner). Supervision of the natives on reserves or stations is the answer to native welfare and this must be forced on the people who employ natives, not as a useful help but as a means of profit.

Everywhere I went I found myself up against strong opposition whenever I mentioned a better spin for the natives. The excuses were 'Spoil the natives', 'Bad enough as it is', 'Never live here' (this apparently from the Casanovas), 'They must die out, leave them alone', 'Don't like vegetables'— (apparently these people have never seen natives dig up a yam).

On the 10th June I returned from Patrol and now submit this report in the hope that something will be done for these unfortunate people, who have carried the full weight of the pastoral industry ever since it started, giving good service to a master who—in most cases—only looks upon them in the same category as the animals that feed upon the runs that were once the tribal area of these people.

A. Patrol Officer Harney
Native Affairs Branch
B. June, 1945
Patrol Officer Report to Native Affairs Branch,
Australian Archives, Darwin

When old Bill Harney came to Willeroo, I can remember him telling people, 'I pushed this road through here in 1932.'

'Oh yeah,' they'd say, 'well there'll be a monument here for you when you'll be goin'.'

He used to always talk to an old bloke called Alf Martin— the boss of VRD from where old Dick Scobie pinched the cattle for old Noel Healey. At that time VRD was owned by Bovril, and old Alf used to say to old Bill, 'What a wonderful job you done here Bill, pushed that road across here with the donkey team, and always had a load of Aborigine workin', givin' you a hand with the crowbar and shovel, rootin' up the big rock and fillin' up the hole with the termite.' They would talk about all this sort of stuff, then old Alf said, 'That your son there?'

My dad would say, 'No, no, no, not mine.'

But in private he was my dad all right. He knew where I was, and every time he came back to Willeroo district he said, 'Hello son,' and say to my mum, 'How's that boy? Show him your history and the story, keep the cultural side going.' He used to give me some lollies, some silver coins. We used to give it to our old mum, and she didn't know what to do with it—she just kept it, on and on and on. Nobody used to spend anything. There was nowhere to spend anything.

Anyway, in front of the white man and with the Welfare blokes my dad didn't want to claim me. He was frightened, because in that time Europeans weren't allowed to be associated with Aboriginals. If you weren't married it was against the law: 'No European was allowed to be associated with an Aboriginal lady.' You could get married if you went into the court and everybody in the government agreed, but for just associating with the Aboriginal lady it was six months' jail and £1000 fine. Anyway, the European bloke couldn't go without it because there was no other white women in the country, but if the Aboriginal woman had a kid to the white man, the Welfare used to go down to the Aboriginal camp and shoot the dogs off the camp, and if the kid was there they asked the old Aboriginal lady, 'Who that kid belong to?'

It doesn't worry us Aborigine if the kid was from another man or woman, it's still our kid. We won't say he's not ours. No one could stop the Aboriginal lady or the European bloke, but when the white man knew that kids were going to be born he just bolted and was gone, and the little baby had no father. Then the Aboriginal bloke, the husband of the lady, he took care of the kid, like Joe Jomornji did with me.

But the Welfare would take the kid away, because that was the law. It was very sad to be taken because the parents were howling and crying their heads off, and the Aborigine couldn't say, 'I gunna keep him 'ere.' He was their kid all right, but because he was half-caste, a different colour from black, they had to let him go. The Welfare didn't want to see so many part-Aborigine kids in the full Aboriginal camp, see, but they was breeding the kid themselves—managers, superintendents, stockmen, jackeroos, Welfare blokes, and Christ knows who else!

At the same time the Welfare were setting up these little places for the half-bloods—compounds they called them—and they put the kids away on some islands and out in the bush, away from the towns. They used that like a prison, and the kid that was in there was learning somebody else's culture.

Then the old Aborigine like Harry Huddleston swung back and they said to the Welfare man, 'You come in here to take the kid away from the parents. That's makin' the people very upset.'

The Welfare turned around and said, 'We can't touch the full-blood kid, but we gotta take them half-caste kid away to put it in a foster home.'

But the Aborigine said, 'What a foster home?'

Welfare said, 'To become educated, so he learn something over there, and he can come back to educate the people.' That's what he told them, but he told them a lie, of course.

I always remember Harry Huddleston saying, 'You mustn't take any kid from this country. This is his home. We reared them kids in the bush country.'

And old Bill was frightened that the Welfare would take me away, and we were frightened too, because my sister Dulcie was taken away, around about 1940, by old Bob Wood, the policeman from Katherine. According to what I was told from my mum, the policeman couldn't take me. 'He's too small,' he said, 'we just take his sister.' Old Bill Harney was on a holiday at the time—somewhere, Brisbane, Sydney, I don't know where. There was no aeroplane at that time and they used to ride a boat around, and the boat dragged on a bit, and by the time old Bill got back Dulcie was gone. He was upset a bit, and of course he couldn't do anything about it because of the law. He couldn't bring her back, and he reckoned, 'Oh well, it doesn't matter, just leave Dulcie over there, and we'll keep Bill under cover.'

So my mum was very strict and careful that I didn't get taken away. She used to get this blackcurrant plum from the bush, and it makes your hair go black. My mum always used to crush the black plum together with a big heap of charcoal and put it all over my skin to make me go black, and when the Welfare would come along I'd be sitting right in the middle of those other blacks, and the Welfare bloke would call out, 'Any yella kids? Any half-caste kids around here?'

'No nothin' 'ere,' but I'd be sitting there with them all painted up black. Of course when the Welfare went away I'd go down the waterhole and dive in the water and I'd come back a half-caste again. I was the only half-caste that wasn't taken away from my mother to the islands, and when they were taken away they were put right outta sight for good.

But funny with my sister Dulcie, she never forgot me. She was at Croker Island, and she remembered where she was from, and my name, and she come back to Katherine around about Christmas time 1950 and looked around. The horseraces were on at the racecourse, and I was over there, and when she heard someone mention my name she come up to me and she told me who she was.

She said, 'You know who I am?'

I said, 'No.' I didn't know her by her body.

She said, 'I'm your sister, Dulcie Harney.'

I said, 'Oh crikey!'

She said, 'I was taken away.'

'Well,' I said to her, 'I knew you went away, and I didn't think you'd ever come back to see me. I'm very pleased that you saw me.'

Then she said, 'What's my mother's name?'

I said, 'Ludi.' She said, 'Where is she, can I see her?'

So I took her over to where our mum was there at the horseraces, and my mother was so pleased and cried for her, and Dulcie put her foot beside my mother's foot and said, 'See, my foot like yours! Look at the toes!' and they looked just the same. They talked for about a week or so, and then Dulcie went back to Darwin, and she used to come back down a lot, and she had kids and used to bring her kids down to see their grandmother. The kids used to visit a lot before old Ludi died.

I remember my sister said, 'I'm the only one that was over on Croker Island that come straight back to my family. All the others was just forgotton, they don't know who they are.'

I said, 'How come?'

She said, 'They think they belong to that country, Croker Island.'

I said, 'Oh!'

See, the Welfare and the government never told the kids where they came from. They should have explained everything to the kids—where they come from, and who their mother was—but they said nothing. They call them 'unknown kids' because they didn't know who they were. Some kids never came home again. Sometimes people might come around looking for their family and I said to them, 'You know who your mum is?'

They said, 'All we know we just come from Wave Hill. Can you tell us who my mum is?'

I said, 'Buggered if I know.'

But Dulcie remembered my name, and that's how she found me. Anyway, Dulcie married a bloke from Melbourne called Hill, and she had three boys and a girl—Warren Hill is a bus driver in Darwin, Christopher is in Sydney or in Melbourne somewhere, and Freddy in Adelaide. Freddy was a Bedwood, because he had a different father again.

But the girl, Elizabeth, was adopted by somebody else in Brisbane when she was a baby. That was in 1959, and when she was grown up she was looking around, chasing up her mother. But what Elizabeth didn't know was her mother Dulcie had died. Dulcie was walking across the Stuart Highway Bridge in Darwin near where Bridge Motors is today, and it was a rainy night, and they didn't have those lights in the street—this was back in 1963—and a car with windscreen wipers that weren't working came by and she got hit in the hip by the car. She didn't die straight away, but I think she had a bruise and arthritis set into it and she died with arthritis.

And Elizabeth, the daughter from Dulcie, she went into some place where they get all the lists of all the people that died, and she saw that Dulcie had three boys, and one little girl, Elizabeth, and she was adopted with somebody in Brisbane. And Elizabeth was hunting around and found that Dulcie had a brother—that's me—and then Elizabeth came and found me. I call her Lizzie, and she's my niece. That was good that she found me.

But I remember another Welfare officer, Ted Evans, he knew who I was because he knew my dad, and he come on the run all around the country trying to get me to take me away.

... at the outbreak of World War Two in 1939 I was a shipping clerk with the Commonwealth Stores Supply and Tender

Board ... and thereby not subject to military call-up or other man-power demands ... with the return to 'civvies' in 1945 I became conscious and sensitive of the non-combative role I had played ... so I began to look around ... and I applied for and was appointed as a Cadet Patrol Officer with the Native Affairs Branch in the Northern Territory ... and took up duty in Darwin in April 1946. The change in my lifestyle was, to say the least, dramatic.

From the unpublished *The Moving Finger*, Ted Evans

Old Ted was really hard out to get me, and he couldn't catch me because he had to ring up the managers before he come, and they'd say, 'I'm coming over there just to see how the Aborigines are.'

Then the managers will say to old Joe Jomornji, 'Come on, Joe, pack up and go out bush, the Welfare are coming. Leave a couple of rootin' horses in the paddock—if he wants to come out here to take young Billy, I'll send him over to ride the rootin' horses from the paddock.' See, many property managers didn't like the Welfare coming around because they were taking a lot of part-Aborigine kids off the land and they were wonderful stockmen, and that's why they didn't want to let any Welfare go in to the stock camp.

Well old Ted Evans turned up, and not a soul of an Aborigine was in the camp. 'Where is the rest of the boys?' he said.

'They are out in the bush, they are all working.'

'How can we get there?'

Then the manager said, 'Oh well, you can get down there and muster up some horses in the paddock over there, then you could jump on one of them and go to the stock camp.' Then old Ted used to go out in the field to bring all these horses in. The horse looked so quiet and they put a saddle on him, and next they jump on, and as soon as they kick him in the ribs of course the horse will root like fuckin' hell! Then Ted Evans will be saying, 'Whoa! Whoa! Whoa!' and the next thing the horse will belt him to hell and old Ted got punted off and that was the end of old Ted—he give up hope.

Anyhow, later on, one day in 1971—I was properly grown up then—I went up to Darwin to have a look around and I went up to the Dolphin Hotel to have a couple of cans of beer. I was sitting down, and another bloke was there, and I'm watching him, and I said, 'That look like old Ted Evans.'

One of them said, 'Yes, that's right. That's him all right.'

'Oh well,' I said, 'I'll go over and say hello to him.'

I went across there and I said, 'Hello Ted, how are you going?'

He looked at me, he said, 'By jeez, I've seen you somewhere.'

I said, 'Yeah, I'm Bill Harney.'

'Oh you, you mongrel!' he said. 'What are you doing in here? You should be back out in the bush. You're not to be anywhere near the town. When I wanted you, I couldn't find you, now you're right on top of me, standing up right here. You're too late, everything's gone now, Welfare's all finished.' That's what old Ted said. 'God, you were a very hard man to catch! Every time I come you weren't there, always been hiding. God, you're a very hard man to catch.'

I just laughed at him. I said, 'You know your name is "*Wudu wurren wujban*"?'

He said, 'What's that?'

' "*Wudu wurren wujban*" means you was a bugger for kidnapping the kids.'

'Oh Jesus, I was really going to put you right away, but I couldn't catch you,' he said. 'Oh well, you're right,' and that's the last I seen of him. I was going to go back and sit down and have a yarn with him when he was living at Humpty Doo, before he died, but I never made it.

Anyway, I think they were still knocking the kids off in 1960, and that's why old Bill Harney was frightened to say he was my father, because he was in Welfare, and it was against Welfare rules to be my dad! So in front of others he would say nothing, but he was still my dad, and he used to come around and treat me like he was my dad. He always said hello and bring a lolly and give my old mum some silver coins—but she never knew what to do with it—and then he used to drive off, and later he'd come back again.

Chapter Twelve

THAT'S THE LAW!

When old Bill used to come around I saw him sitting down with the old blokes, and he used to listen to stories from them for his books. He was asking old Pluto and Joe about the history of Aboriginal life, and the songs, and the story for the country. The first time I went to sit down with him, they told old Bill, 'That young bella comin', don't talk about it,' and that pencil and paper they put under the blanket. Then they sang out to me, 'You go away young bella, go away, not allowed,' and as soon as I'd go they start again. This was ceremony law they were telling old Bill, and you can't know this until you've been through initiation, and learnt about your Dreaming. Grade one in the school was when Joe Jomornji taught us how to hunt kangaroo and emu, later on, the Dreaming, that is like grade two. Joe really knew a lot of Aboriginal law, and with my grandfathers and uncles he was the old man that passed on to me the stories from the Dreaming.

Now, for the European, in the white man's way, your father's tombstone, that's your Dreaming—that's what's left behind in the cemetery. Well that's the way our Dreaming is—what our grand, grand, grandparents passed on to our grandfather and fathers, all the way right up to us. We call that Dreaming *Buwarraja*, and you start to learn about that with your initiation.

I was about twelve maybe, in about 1948, and Joe Jomornji and old Pluto said to me, 'Your Dreamin', your totem, is *bulyan* the wedge-tail eagle—not the brown wedge-tail, the jet black one,' and they showed me the wedge-tail eagle painting in the rock. They said that Bulyan the wedge-tail eagle was once a human like us, and his body was painted up with the design of the wedge-tail eagle, and one day Bulyan became a wedge-tail eagle and he flew away.

Then they told me that in the early days, just as the land was coming out of the water to be the land, all the different birds and animals were just like you and me—human—and they showed us the caves with the paintings of the Lightning Brothers, and they told us how back when water was everywhere, the Lightning Men were the first men in this country, painted up like the Lightning Men in the rock. They said, 'We call this country *Jankangyina* country—that means we have the Lightning Brothers paintings everywhere, all over the country. The main one is called *Jabiringa* and he makes the rain in the country, and the other one *Yagdjagbula*, he strikes the lightning all over the country.'

Then Joe and all my other uncles told us how *Jabiringa* and *Yagdjagbula* were in the country and the Rainbow Snake was there too. The Rainbow Serpent was the one who had brought all the water into the country, he pushed the sea across, and sang the water to go higher and higher, and everywhere was water. The country was just one big flood, and everybody had to move from the low place up to the high place, and lots of Lightning Men were based on the high place too.

The willie-wagtail was operating in the country then—he was human like us then, and now he's a bird today—and he was building up the high places for people to live there, and he found all the spearheads in the country. He said to the Lightning Men, 'Look, this water is still rising, maybe we can get the spears and we can kill the Rainbow Snake?'

The Lightnings said, 'Okay, we'll go ahead and try.' They put the spearheads together, and the first spear the Lightning Man threw chopped the old Rainbow Snake in half but never killed him. The second spear the Lightning Man threw chopped the old Rainbow Snake in half again, but still never killed him.

At the same time, two other birds that was human like us—that's the brown falcon, *girrgany*, and the peregrine falcon, *barnangaya*—they threw a spear from Mt Gregory in the Gregory National Park—in Wardaman that place is *Wunangai*—and that spear came right across the country and landed on the back of the Rainbow Snake and chopped his head right off. The head of the Rainbow Snake fell down, and the eyeballs flew out and landed 5 kilometres away, and they became the waterholes over there called *Yimum*. Then the water disappeared right back to where the sea level is now, and all this country was just bare. Now today, when I take the Jankangyina Tours to my country, I show them the big long rock that is the old Rainbow Serpent lying there, with his head hanging off the end.

Anyway, the land was cleared of all the water and the old Lightning Man reckoned, 'That's good. Let's go down and start hunting for food.'

So they all went down hunting, but a lot of them were getting perished. They said, 'We want water, we're getting perished.'

The Lightning said, 'All right, I can make water for us to drink, I will sing that rain.'

Then the black-headed python came along and said to the Lightning Man, 'Look, when you sing that rain, the cloud will go up, and when he burst all the water will come down and will just run away. We must have rivers in this country to hold the water.'

The Lightning Man said, 'Well how we gunna make the river?'

The black-headed python said, 'Well I got a digging stick here, called *milirri*.'

'Oh!' said the Lightning Man. 'All right, we'll wait for you to make the river.'

Well that digging stick was like dynamite. He's got electricity inside that *milirri*, and the black-headed python along with the water python went ahead and they cut all the rivers in the country. They named everything as they travelled, and made all the big gorges, and all the little channels, and they made the songline that gives all the names for every place on the path they travelled. That's the sacred song we sing called *gudinja*. It follows where the python went, and that's passed on to us now, from the beginning. And when they had finished they came back and said, 'Well there you are, all the rivers are there now. They need to be filled.'

The Lightning said, 'All right.'

He already had a hole dug in the ground, and he picked up his number seven boomerang—it's got a bend on him like a 7—and just before he started to sing, the grasshopper came along and said to the old Lightning, 'Look, when you sing the rain, the cloud will go up in the air and he'll only float in one spot, he won't move.'

The Lightning said, 'How we gunna make it move?'

The grasshopper said, 'Well I got a song here to make a whirly-wind.'

The Lightning said, 'All right, we'll sing together,' and the Lightning Man picked up his number seven boomerang and started singing. The cloud started to build up, and the grasshopper was singing over his end, and the old whirly-whirly went up in the air and picked up all the cloud and spread it all over the country. At the same time, the Lightning Man threw the boomerang and hit the cloud and thunder went off and the rain come down. He rained for week, flooded, and when the rain stopped, all the rivers were full.

Next, the black-headed python come along and said to the old Lightning Man, 'Well there you are, you did a good job, you made all the water. And look at what I did, there's a river now, all the rivers are full. Everybody can have a drink.' They were pleased with themselves, and all over the country there was water. But everything was moving—there was no rock, it was all just mud—and all the trees were moving in the mud.

Anyway, there was one dog there, called *mudburongo*, and he was chasing the kangaroos all over the place, and one little boy was there who was the son of the Lightnings, human like us, he started to follow the trail for that dog. All the Lightning Men were yelling out to this little boy not to get close by the dog, and the little boy wasn't taking any notice at all. He continued on and after a while he saw the dog laying down there. He yelled out to the dog, and the dog never moved. He said, 'The dog must be dead.'

All them little Lightning Men they were sitting in all this mud, and they were yelling out to the little boy, 'Don't get close by the dog, otherwise the dog will eat you.' Then the little boy looked down on the ground and he saw these flints. He picked up one of these flints. He yelled out to the dog, and the dog never moved. 'Well,' he said, 'the dog must be dead. If I slit the dog's ears he might wake up.'

Before he slit the dog's ears everything in this country was moving. All the Lightnings were humans like us, walking around in this mud, painted up in the design for the Lightning, and as soon as that little boy slit the dog's ears the dog screamed, and everything come to a standstill in the country, and the soft high mountain changed to become a rock. Today it's a rock formation, and when the mud became rock these Lightning Brothers got frozen in the rock, and they are still there today, about 2 metres high.

Jabiringa is the one that makes the very big rain we call *barrawurnd*—cyclone—and the other one, *Yagdjagbula*, he's the one that strikes all the trees with lightning. Now we got to watch out for him when it's raining, because old Joe told us never use the axe when the rain comes, because the lightning will come down and hit that axe and kill you.

And when that mud turned to rock, that's when Bulyan, my totem, the wedge-tail eagle, turned from a human into a bird—he just flew into the soft mud wall and that's where he stayed, and later, when this mud became hard, Bulyan became the rock painting we look at today, like the Lightning Brothers. We didn't paint the rocks to start with—all the paintings are just the many animals who put themselves into the rock in the Dreaming times, the *Buwarraja*, and today we just touch the paintings up every now and again to keep them going.

Anyhow, old Joe and my uncles showed me Bulyan, and

then when the flowers came on the coolibah in September, the circumcision time had come, and it came time for my ceremony for me to be made into a man.

First they sent me walking across to Manbulloo where lots of my relations were, walking all the way, painted up in red ochre. I was called *warling*—that's your name before your circumcision—and I wore a little hair belt with a little pearl shell and a white cockatoo feather on the belt.

When I got to Manbulloo I had to round up all of my relations to follow me back to Willeroo to do my circumcision for me. Now to muster them up I had the bark off the white gum tree, and I hit them with that bark, and then they came back to Willeroo with me—some Daguman blokes, a bit of Wardaman, some Jawoyn. I put the muster on them and away we went, all the way, and I was sitting behind them, driving them with the bark. Every morning I threw the bark at them by the fire place, making them wake up quick, and as they're travelling they yell out all the way, like a steam train: 'Aaaaooooaaaah Aaaaooooaaaah Aaaaooooaaaah.' They make that noise all the way for the spiritual side. It echoes all the way up to the atmosphere and the young fella doesn't get sick. I wasn't making a noise, I was just the driver, from Manbulloo all the way right up to Willeroo, to this big ring place, and when they got there they all sat there till the cool time in the afternoon.

Then in the evening my dad, old Joe Jomornji, got blood from his vein and he put the blood on me and stuck feathers all over me, and they painted my body with the design for the wedge-tail eagle. They said, 'This is the design you goin' to use, this is yours,' and the men wrapped me all around with a big paperbark because no one's allowed to see me.

All my family and all our Wardaman mob are all sitting there waiting, and the men bring me across just about four o'clock in the afternoon, and they're all singing and dancing all the way. All my family are there just sitting down, and when we get close, one of them will walk up and open up the paperbark, and there's me standing up right in the middle. Then they'll all come right down close by to see the different designs I've got. I'm standing up in the middle, and they dance, and then they made me sit down next to my mum and dad. They cry for me then, because I'd been a month away to Manbulloo, and I look me so pretty, and they feel sorry for me. Then they have a drink of tea, and all the old ladies go away, and the men dance all night. Only men, all night, non-stop. That dance is called *lirrga*, with all the didgeridoos and the clap sticks.

Then next day they gave a call for the women, and I was put with the women. They danced and sang the *bundimi*, but I was not allowed to see the women dancing. I was buried all night with the blanket over my face. Doesn't matter if I'm hot, I can suffocate, that's all right. I just lay there, quiet.

Then all the women picked up a firestick—they call that *wujunggu*—and they threw it up in the air like a shooting star, and they all yelled, 'Oooooooooooh tush!', and the firestick he fell down. That means that with circumcision I wouldn't get any infection and pus around my body. Then all the old ladies brought me back to the men, and the old boys started again, singing that *gudinja* all night.

That's the third night now, and they danced for me. I had to sit up there all night to watch, no sleep at all. They won't tell you what they're going to do to you, and I thought it was just for fun. You think they're just singing a song, and you just clap like one of them because it makes you feel happy. They dance till breaking dawn, and as soon as it's light enough to see, six old men lie flat on the ground like a table, belly down. Then one boy hung on to me, and he lay on top of them and I'm on top of that boy—he's got his leg over me, and his two arms around me, holding on.

It's just breaking dawn and they call out with another song which was invented by the willie-wagtail, and then they come along with that stone knife. I didn't know what was going on. I thought they were going to strangle me at first, but you're not allowed to sing out, and they all yell 'Waaaaaa!' like this, and they nick the skin off at the same time, and I was circumcised. With the stone knife it makes the skin go numb, and you can't feel it cut off. Then they put the skin in a paperbark and hid him away. When I stood up, all my brothers-in-law were still laying down there with their belly down and all the blood was dripping on their backs. Then one of them took me away into the shade and gave me feed and water. Then after that I went to sleep straight away.

Then later when it healed up, one of my friends came along to check on me. That's when they said, 'Well, young fella all right now,' but I wasn't allowed to go into the water to have a swim till the storm came around about Christmas time. This all happened down at Ingaladi waterhole where my tour camp is today. They waited till the floodwaters came running and then two blokes jumped in the water and they sang and blew the didgeridoo in the middle of the floodwater. They played a very big good didgeridoo with a good sound on it—none of these shop ones—and a good blower on it too.

We call that song *mamurrng*, and the Rainbow Serpent who lives under the water can hear it saying, 'We're bringing a kid across now to make him clean, so don't do any harm to him.' See, I still had the ochre on me from the circumcision. Then they put a blindfold on me and raced flat out and dived me in this floodwater. They hung onto me for a few minutes underneath the water, and when I was all clean again the Rainbow Serpent will say, 'Well, that's good now,' and I could go and dive in any river, and swim around picking up turtles, no problem. But if they didn't clean me up and tell the Rainbow Serpent, the Rainbow can smell all the ochre stuff, and he'll say. 'Oh, this one hasn't got cleaned off, we'll drown him.'

They called me *yaba* after that, I was no longer a *warling*. From there you go right through till you become a proper man, and they'll call him *marlu*, and when we became a *marlu* they drafted us out then. The black one went to get the cuts on the arm and the chest, but the part-Aborigine like me didn't get any tribal mark, because when a lot of half-castes were taken away with the Welfare, the white man will ask, 'What's the mark for?' and you can't tell about the tribal law. So only the black one get the tribal mark.

Then Joe Jomornji and old Pluto told us how the Lightnings gave us water in this country, that they made the law too. They told us that the Lightnings said, 'We're gunna make a very good strong law, and he's got to stay that way. This law is going to be passed down from our time to generation to generation.' The Lightnings made the law about that stone knife for the initiation, and the dog who screamed when his ears got cut, he made the bigger law for the next ceremony, and that's the law called 'whistle-cock'.

See, before the dog screamed everyone was like a dog when he had sex—his dick got knotted up and he can't get out—but when that dog screamed, he changed to become a spiritual devil-dog called *lugoro*, and he made the law for the whistle-cock.

Now whistle-cock we call *ijor*, and it is where they split the prick with a stone knife or a razor, right down the bottom of the cock, slow, bit by bit, all along underneath, and his eye goes blue with the pain. That's sacred from the initiation, the whistle-cock, and the prick looks like a sausage when she splits. With the whistle-cock, when you piss you can hear it whistling. It's like the opening of a tap—whissssh! And the girls like it. That's what it's meant for. It's supposed to give you a good flavour—flavour is what we mean for feeling, flavour is really in love—both come together, both come in a hurry. They made this whistle-cock because it was a good flavour between the man and the woman—the noises of the suction between the man and the woman is like they are getting bogged in mud and coming out and that makes a thrill and makes it all come quicker, and then you can do it a second, and a third one will take a bit longer then, but he'll make a hell of a racket! You won't want to be close by other people listening to you—you have to be away about 10 mile away!

And again, it's just like putting a condom on you. It just flows out underneath, and that's a method of stopping a baby, and I remember a time when the Welfare blokes Ted Edmondson and Charlie Sweeny come along, and they had a doctor with them. They come along asking if any Aborigine in the bush had a disease. They told us about how they were looking after and supporting Aboriginal people, and said, 'You take your shirt off. The doctor going to have a look at you, so he can see if you got leprosy, or any other different disease.'

They're looking at our chest, and they see the scars on the chest from the initiation, and they see the hole in the nose, and they put that down on the paper. And they get down to have a look to see if we had any TB, and they're looking around the old fella's cock, and the doctor could see where the old Aborigine had a whistle-cock.

The doctor he said, 'Hello,' he said, 'what's this down the bottom here? What do you split it down here for? Were you born like this?'

I remember old Harry Huddleston saying, 'No, we gotta have a mark in the chest, we gotta have a hole in the nose, we gotta have a whistle-cock. When we got this we proper man. If you got none of that you're not a man. That's our law,' and Harry pointed to the doctor and the Welfare men. 'You only a little boy yet.'

'No,' he said, 'no, we not little boy.'

'Yeah, you still a little boy.'

'What makes you think that?'

'Because you gotta have that mark on the chest, and the nose, and you gotta have that whistle-cock, then you're a man. That's in the law.'

'But I'm a man.'

'No you're not, because you've got skin on, you're not circumcised, you're still a little boy.'

'But I'm an old man!'

'I know,' and old Harry was laughing, 'you old, but only little boy. You must have this whistle-cock before you can be a proper man.'

Then the doctor said, 'Can I stitch you up?'

Harry said, 'No, you break the law. We've got to have this to be a man.'

'Oh,' the doctor said, 'I'll have to take you in to get it stitched up.'

Then one other old boy said, 'You can't stitch him up! That's the law! The law has been left to us and we gotta keep that!' And they kept it that way.

Then the Welfare blokes and the doctor must have gone over and told the missionary bloke about the whistle-cock, and the Inland Missionary bloke come out to talk to the Aborigine about not splitting the cock any more, and no more putting on the initiation, and no more marking around the chest and shoulders, and putting a hole in the nose. They're saying, 'Only devil do that, you gotta throw your ceremony away. Come our Christian way. You believe in God and all this and you be a man.'

All our mob, all the old people, they turned around and said, 'We are men, but you're not. You might be missionary,' they said, 'but you not a man, you still a boy. We don't want to listen to you, Christian,' they said, 'we got our law over here'.

Then Harry and the others they go over to the homestead and tell the manager, 'The Christian bloke here gunna tell us what to do, we don't want him,' and the managers came down and told him to shove off and he never got near us again.

Anyhow, each year I attended the law, all the way to the bigger ceremonies, and I've got lots of the Dreaming songs and the secret songs. I've got a song from all the animals, and we've got songs for sweethearts, and songs for making the rain come, and songs for making the rain stop. That song for singing the rain is another type of *yarrindi* song. They don't teach you that *yarrindi* when you're a kid because it could be dangerous—you could sing it and destroy a lot of things. I never got around to singing that *yarrindi* to make the rain. I missed out on that one because later I went up from the Aboriginal camp into the white camp to learn to be a stockman. That's when one bloke from the white camp, old Clarrie Wilkinson, told me about how old Sambo sang the *yarrindi* at Wave Hill.

Chapter Thirteen

SINGING THE RAIN

This old bloke Clarrie Wilkinson was at Wave Hill Station back in about 1920, and everything was getting dried up and the spring water that used to last all the year round was a dry well. All the cattle used to get bogged and just died, and all the old drovers were just lying down there on the side of the creek waiting for rain—they needed the water to move on with the cattle.

Anyway, old Clarrie Wilkinson said to one of these Aboriginal boys, old Sambo, 'I heard a lot of you old blackfellas can sing in the rain?'

Sambo said, 'Yeah, I can sing it for you, old fella, make all the river run.'

'Well,' old Charlie Wilkinson said to this boy, 'if you can do that, I'll give you tobacco and some flour and some tea and sugar and look after you with the tin fruit.'

He said, 'All right.'

Clarrie said, 'I'll put away for you one side of corned beef because I want to see you go down and sing the rain.'

And Sambo said, 'All right, I'll go down and do that.'

Anyway, all the drovers, Mick Cussens and Owen Cummins and old Charlie Swan and Jack Chuckabull, were down the river, and away Sambo went up the river to Catfish. He sang that *yarrindi*, and a few days after down the rain come! He sang a great big storm and that night a big rain come down the river and flooded the drover's camp right out, and swept the old homestead away! The homestead got swiped right off! Everything was in flood. There was no more homestead, and everybody cleared up to the hill, and the rain stopped running and the water was full, everywhere.

Anyway this old blackfella, old Sambo, when he heard the Wave Hill homestead got swiped, he wasn't game to come back to see old Clarrie to get his bag of flour and sugar and tea. Old Mick Cussens the drover was very disappointed because all his cattle got swiped away by the floodwater, and old Owen Cummins and old Charlie Swan and Jack Chuckabull and all them was very disappointed that all their droving gear was washed away by floodwater—they had no more gear to be drovers. Old Mick Cussens got drunk and he said, 'Where is that old Sambo? I ever run into that Sambo that sang that rain, I'll shoot him and feed him to the goats.'

Then they goes over and tells old Sambo. 'Sambo,' they says, 'old Mick Cussens's gunna shoot you and gunna feed you to the goats.' That frightened old Sambo and he kept on going.

Then old Clarrie Wilkinson the manager come down and said, 'Oh that's very good! I didn't tell him to sing a big rain to wash the homestead away! I only wanted a bit of water around the bed of the creek to water the cattle.' He said, 'Tell the old fella to come 'round so I can give him a feed now, to give him all this flour and tea and sugar.'

Well the other Aborigines were hunting around and they found old Sambo all right, and they told him to come around and get tea and sugar, but this old boy he got fright because he sang too much water and took half the homestead away, so he never turned up. He kept on going with fright, and he finished down at Hooker Creek somewhere.

Anyway, old Clarrie Wilkinson borrowed a bit of a tent and rigged up this tent, and old Clarrie said to one of those boys, 'If you ever run into old Sambo, tell him to come back and get some of his flour. No need for him to be frightened after he sang the rain that swiped the station off and a lot of the old drovers lost their camp.'

Anyway, gradually they started building Wave Hill homestead up again. A lot of the old blacks come back from the desert and were all settled in there in Wave Hill, and all the drovers got some new gear and they carried on.

And for me, old Clarrie Wilkinson used to always sit

down and talk about this thing. *Yijunda* Wilkinson he was called—that means the stumpy one—and he told me lots of things, and he wanted to look after me. I was still living with my mother in the Aboriginal camp on Willeroo, and Clarrie wanted to adopt me. He had no sons, he had no wife, nothing. He really took a liking to me, and he classed me like a son. My father, old Bill Harney, had left the Welfare and I didn't run into him much after that. I heard he was based in Darwin, somewhere near Two Fella Creek, close to Rum Jungle somewhere. I knew some old Malak boys—very long, tall fellas—they used to talk about him a lot. There were lots and lots of Aborigines living in that country and he sat down and based with them like he did all over in this country. Anyhow, I've never been there—I just knew it was somewhere about Mandorah.

> Bill Harney Snr retired from the Native Affairs Branch in 1948, erected a tin hut under a banyan tree at Durramunkamunni, by a lagoon on Two Fella Creek on the Cox Peninsula, twenty kilometres from Darwin across Darwin Harbour, and remained there writing and beachcombing until 1957.
>
> Jan Wositzky

Anyway, Clarrie Wilkinson would have been about seventy, sixty, I suppose, and I was only a little fella, about twelve, and he knew I was full of go. Then when I moved on into the stock camp, old Clarrie began to rear me up. He wanted to make a good man out of me—which he did, he made a real man out of me—and he was going to make me into a leader, and that's what I became—a supervisor in the stock camp.

Chapter Fourteen

A LITTLE STOCKMAN

All part-Aboriginal employees are in receipt of award rates of pay, Bill Harney receiving wages applicable to a youth under eighteen years of age. Bill is still in the Willeroo stock camp, it being claimed that he would not receive sufficient experience with the Manbulloo camp. It is claimed that he is being treated as a 'white' but I did not observe him either at work or in camp and am unable to confirm this.

22.8.50
E.C. Evans
PATROL OFFICER
'Report on Manbulloo, Willeroo and Delamere Stations', from Ted Evans to Native Affairs Branch,
Australian Archives, Darwin

I would a been ten year old when I started to become to be a little stockman. The first horse I rode was I think in 1945. I was only a very small fella, and we used to get dressed up with a little cowboy hat and big baggy trousers and boots, and away we'd go riding a horse. My old man Joe Jomornji always stuck by me, like Clarrie, seeing that I didn't fall off the horse and get hurt. The other kids were the same, their parents were looking after them, and we had to catch the horses for the stockmen so that they can take off mustering cattle.

We were the horse tailer, and after that we were what they call a bullock tailer—you let the cattle out of the yard, and take him to have a feed in the grass. When all the cattle go to sleep you go over to the camp and have your lunch, and soon as the cattle all feed up then get up, you take them down the water and water them. Then you bring them back and let them have one more feed. By that time it's just sundown and you take them in and yard them up. That's what a bullock tailer does, and I went down there bullock tailing and growing up, about eleven or twelve year old.

Then we were starting to go out and muster wild cattle in the bush. We used to take off in April and we'd ride out from the homestead. If there were three hundred in the community there could be anything up to twenty-five to thirty ride out to the stock camp, just looking around for any wild cattle.

And in the stock camp there'd be two bosses—the Aboriginal one and your European boss, the supervisor. So when the cattle were hid in the scrub, the supervisor had to work in with the Aborigine and take instructions from the Aborigine because the Aborigine knows the country, and can tell the supervisor where the cattle are. But if this supervisor wanted to take off on his own without asking the Aborigine which way to muster, then there'll always be an upset. The Aborigine would know that there's no cattle over there and they'll be riding with nothing happening, and the next thing that supervisor bloke would be getting bored and getting wild and start snapping at somebody. Of course the Aborigine would swing back and go to tell the manager boss at the homestead, 'He not asking where the cattle are. You know we can't explain it to him unless he ask,' and the boss bloke would come along and boot the supervisor out because he wouldn't fit in with the Aborigine.

Anyhow, first of all I wasn't really chasing the cattle in the bush, I was only just driving the coachers—a coacher is cattle that is quiet, tame. We let the coachers out of the yard about half past four in the morning—that's just beginning of daylight—and we'll drive the coachers out into the bush. There was no fencing in that country, and when you came across the cattle you let go last year and the new unbranded calves, they're wild and they get a fright and take off.

Then one lot of stockmen would split off and chase them over the gullies and up the hill and down the hill, and bring them in behind the coachers. Once they sat the wild cattle with the quieter cattle, then you could drive them back to the yard no problem. If you didn't have the coachers the wild cattle would not be able to stand still, because they're wild and they're likely to go off any minute. Anyway, we'd bring them back at sunset to the yard in the bush, and the head stockman, he'd say, 'We gunna brand first thing in the morning.'

So we were back to being old horse tailer again, and we put the bell on the bronco horse and let him go for the night. The bronco horse is a very big horse and he pulls the calf along to get branded. Then early in the morning the horse tailer goes out to pick up the bronco horse. He walks along and listens for the bell jingling, and he walks straight up and brings the bronco horse back to the camp. By that time, about four o'clock, all the other boys had their breakfast and they'll be down the yard lighting the fire to get the branding iron hot. Then down the yard the blokes start lassoing the calf with the rope, and the bronco horse brings the calf up, and two persons lasso the front leg and the hind leg, and the calf falls over. One man races across and puts the brand on the calf, and another bloke will split his ears—that split ears tells you that he's branded. If you don't split their ears it's what they call a clean-skin, and anyone else can claim it. Then another bloke will castrate him, and then they let the calf go with the cows to the main hole and water them. We take them out on the flat and steady them down. There the cows and calf can mother up, and then as soon as everything is settled, we used to walk away and leave.

Not like today, they do it opposite. They dive-bomb the cattle with the helicopter and startle them right back to the homestead. After they brand the cows and calves in the yard, they open the gates and the cows go flat out one way and the calves go one other way, and the mother is looking for her calf and she can't find this calf because the dingo comes along, eats the calf. In our time we used to saddle the cow and calf together, mother them up, and that way the old cow always had control over the little calf.

Then if we shot a cow for beef we always saved the hide. Joe Jomornji would say, 'I want that hide to make rope,' and he gets a pocket knife and cuts it up into three strands and when we got that all twisted up, Joe would splice a bull-hide rope, and we used that rope for lassoing the calf, and that's how I learnt to be a stockman. Joe Jomornji was out there teaching me all the time. He was a very good stockman—good horseman, good musterer, good at making ropes, hobbles, good at building yard fences and breaking in horses. At operating the cattle, he's the man.

And old Clarrie Wilkinson was there too, a wonderful old man, and he wanted me to be a leader. He didn't force me, but he showed me a lot of stuff—making hobbles and making ropes, and he showed me the organisation of the cattle. He'd say, 'When you're running the camp, never force yourself. Don't try and jump at people who work for you, just talk to them, organise them neatly, rightly, and take the lead. They'll follow you.' He said, 'A lot of people are making mistakes and scream at them, roar at them. No one will like that. That's where all the confusion and fight come in.' That's what he said.

But in those times in the stock camp, many of the European blokes were cruel to us, swinging us onto bad horses, and if we didn't do what they told us, we got flogged with the whip. In the freezing cold morning we had to ride the horses with bare feet, and in the branding yard they didn't give a damn if we get horned by the bullock. They always said, 'Get in that yard!' We was frightened of the yard, but we got chucked in with the savage bullock.

See in those times it was very hard, and these days, everything's very easy—Aboriginal people got easy life, white people got easy life, yella fellas got easy life. But when I was a kid it was very tough and hard. Everybody was copping it, but we didn't want to escape from that district because we belong to the area. This was Wardaman country, and so we just stayed there all the time.

I remember seeing one old fella called Tom Liddy in a bronco yard throw a rope over the head of this blackfella and start dragging him in amongst the savage bullocks in the yard, and Tom Liddy reckoned it was great fun.

Tom Liddy had a bit of a property around Moil, and he got on to a lot of these wild blacks and they shot a lot of them out and took a helluva lot back for work. A few of them run away, and they chased them to bring them back. Well, old Tom Liddy was a hard man on Aboriginal people, and he said to the boys, 'Take your boot off. Come over here,' and he tied them with a chain to the tree. Then he was rasping the sole of their feet with a rasp, crippling them up, to make sure they can't run away. Old Tom Liddy was just sitting down laughing, he reckoned it was a great joke. One time he tied a man on a bolting horse with a surcingle over his leg and let the horse go bush.

One other fella when I started was called Colin—I can't remember his second name—and he was a very hard man. We had to go to sleep just on the sunset and be asleep straight away—none of this talking business. If we did talk, well, he'd grab our heads and bash our heads together, and if we didn't get up in the morning early, then he'd grab our feet and throw us in the waterhole, or he'd put a shovelful of hot coals and ashes over our blanket.

Just to show you how hard he was, one day when we were mustering out in the stock camp, Blucher, my cousin, and I went down to get a drink of water from the canteen, and this Colin grabbed me and put my head in a billy of water and nearly drowned me. I don't know what he did that for, and of course my old dad Joe Jomornji was very upset. He didn't say anything till later when we drafted a lot of cattle up across at Brandy Bottle Creek, where I was born, and we were racing around after some very raw horses on the flat, and we couldn't catch them, and this Colin's yelling out to one other boy, 'Go on, throw the rope on him and pull him in.'

The boy was saying, 'Aah, it's very hard. We're getting buggered now trying to bring that horse in,' and old Colin got real niggly and hit this other boy.

Of course then a lot of older Aborigines took our place and fired back at the European bloke, 'You mustn't do that cruelness to the kids!' Then another Aborigine called Albert came across and they had a fight. Albert was a brother of old Tarpot, who was Joe Jomornji's nephew, and Tarpot came along and threw great big rock across and hit Colin on the chest and broke his chest inside, and it caved in on his heart and put him out of plumb. He was out. They ended up bringing him back to Willeroo, and brought him to Katherine, and I think he died after that.

Then another bloke called Stumpy Edmondson come along. He was just a relieving stockman in the camp, and it happened one time that there was a buffalo came in among the horses. One of the boys saw this buffalo and said, 'There's a buffalo over there, old man, in the field.'

Old Stumpy said, 'Oh well, we'll go over and get rid of this buffalo,' and he and my other old stepfather, old Nugget Jinamugurru, picked up a .303 and shot this buffalo just on sunset. According to old Nugget, when they walked over to get the horns off the buffalo they couldn't see any mark of any sort on the buffalo—not even a bullet hole—and the buffalo was as dead as a dodo.

Nugget had a funny feeling. He said to Stumpy, 'Hey, that's not a buffalo, that's a human.'

Stumpy Edmondson said, 'What do you mean, it's a human?'

'Well,' Nugget said, 'the spirit of a dead fella come across looking to kill the fella that killed him in the first place.'

'He's a buffalo,' said Stumpy. 'Just take the horns off him,' and they took the horns off.

That night we were all sitting around and I could hear the old boys saying, 'That buffulo was a human all right.' They didn't know where that spirit came from but they did recognise what the buffalo was up to, and we found out the story for that buffalo a little while later.

See, before this, one man from Victoria River Downs had come over to Manbulloo and at Manbulloo he got killed by some other bloke. His parents at VRD were very upset and they teed up one snake singer to destroy this person at Manbulloo, because they found out who he was. Now this snake singer over at VRD took some hair from the dead fella and he sang that hair with a secret song that made that spirit of the dead fella become a snake. Then he put that hair into a termite nest, and again he sung that hair, that spirit, and he called out the name of the man the spirit was going to kill, the guilty one—we call this guilty one *marn girriny*. Then they waited for night-time, and when a shooting star came over in the sky, they knew that the snake would take off under the ground looking for the guilty one, the *marn girriny*.

Now they sang this snake to change himself to become anything—he can become a kangaroo or an echidna, he can change as he is travelling—and this snake was travelling from VRD right up till he came up to Willeroo. What pulled him up there in the first place was this bloke Colin getting hit with the rock. Then the snake changed himself to become a buffalo and he was checking whether the killer he was after was around there. 'Oh, there's no one here that I wanted,' he said, 'might be further over,' but the Aborigines spotted this buffalo standing up looking amongst the horses—that's when Stumpy shot the buffalo.

So this snake reckoned that Stumpy was the *marn girriny* now, the guilty one, and next day Stumpy Edmondson caught a great big bay horse, a very good quiet horse, and they were bringing lots of cattle in to Willeroo to dip. Me and Blucher, my cousin, were driving the cattle, and Stumpy was just riding along beside, and he picked up tobacco out of his pocket and started rolling a cigarette. Then he lit the cigarette and started to smoke. As he started to smoke he passed a termite nest the same as the termite nest the snake singer put the hair inside when he sang the song to kill the *marn girriny*, and that quiet horse took fright and started rooting like buggery and threw Stumpy up in the air and down on the termite nest. The horse was bucking on top of him and every bone was squashed and broken to pieces.

Well, they carried old Stumpy across from there back to Willeroo, and of course there was no motor car or aeroplane of any sort in that time, and it ended up that one of them

raced all the way to Manbulloo to get someone down with
a car to pick him up. He still survived a bit. He had all the
broken bones and they took him down south, and he's been
a crippled man ever since, but he never knew about that *marn
girriny*.

One other white man was very cruel to the Aborigine. Matter
of fact, he poisoned some Aborigines when I was in the
stock camp. This man he didn't like one old stepfather of
mine, old Jack Jarribirdi, because before, in about 1939, they
were both working at a place together, and of course old
Jack was tougher than this white man and in a brawl he beat
him. Then later on Jack ended up working with him again,
and they were out in the mustering camp and this man threat-
ened old Jack with a revolver. Jack had all his other cousins
there—like Bloomer and Dodger and his other brother and
all that mob—and they all got stuck into this man and they
beat him up. After they came home, of course, they were
proud of what they did to him, but that white man said to
himself, 'Well, I'm not going to give in. I'll get around to
getting some of these blokes.'

So he said to the stock camp cook—he was a white man
too—he said, 'Well, you make curry and rice, separate the
good curry onto some plates for us and the kids, and you can
make a bad curry for this mob that beat me up.' He said, 'Put
some strychnine on it,' which the cook did.

So the cook made up the big curry and rice at the
Ingaladi waterhole, and after we finished branding that
morning, Blucher and I went across to the cook and they
told us not to eat this stew—they had ours separate, in different plates. Of course old Harry Huddleston and all that
mob came down and picked up this food and were eating,
they were hungry, and some of them was getting giddy
around the head. They said, 'Oh, the stew got a bit of strychnine. We've got to race down and start eating the mud to
cure the strychnine,' and they raced down to the billabong
and picked up some mud and started eating the mud. A lot

of them were putting their hand in the mouth and they brought all the food out, and the mud dissolved all the strychnine and cleared them out.

But two others, old boys, my other old stepfather Jack and old George Donnelly, they got in a little bit too deep. Those two boys got badly poisoned. My old stepfather, old Jack, he didn't want to bring anything out, he continued on eating it, and of course, they got real crook and then they had to bring them into Willeroo. Old George Donnelly pulled through, but my old stepfather, old Jack Jarribirdi, he got crook and died, died for good, finished up.

Anyway, that white man, he went across and worked at another place, over to the west. While he was down there, they couldn't catch him, but he and the owner of the place had a fight over something, and he got beaten. I was told about it when I was there at the same place working in the 1960s. I was told that that white man, he went down to Perth, and I never heard any more about him.

Another cook at that time was Knock-'em-Down Tommy Cody, and when he came, oh! he was a very crabby thing, and my cousin Kaiser was telling me about him because he knew him. 'See that old man over there, that Tommy Knock-'em-Down?' he said.

I said, 'Yeah, why do they call him Knock-'em-Down Tommy?'

'Oh,' he said, 'they call him Knock-'em-Down Tommy because every time he fought somebody he knocked them down.' He was mates to nobody, and he was very savage. They used to call him 'Handle Bar' too, because he had a huge big moustache. He wasn't a gun cook, just good enough to race around and cook in the stock camp, and when he was cooking in the stock camp you wasn't allowed to go anywhere near the kitchen fireplace. But one cold morning, being that I was only a stupid young fella, I went across to squat down near the fireplace. I didn't realise it was the cook's fire, and when I squatted down he picked up a shovelful of coal and spread it on top of me, all over, and I got all burnt, and I didn't go near his fire after that.

We were only about twelve years old and we were frightened that we'd get flogged with the whip. And later, of course, when I came to be a stockman, I was spreading the coal on the young kids' blanket like they done it to me. Not only me, all the others were the same, all over. Oh, it was hard then, but today you can't tell a young Aboriginal bloke what to do, they just laugh at you. But we were bought up the hard way, and we went along, learning at the same time.

Anyway, after he burnt me with the ashes, one day the supervisor told Tom Cody to bake a cake, and Tom Cody says, 'If youse want a cake, I'll soon make you a cake.'

Well he goes over and makes a soggy cake. Oh jeez, she was real soggy. He never put any cream of tartar or soda in it, just Epsom salts. Smoko time comes and he gave them the cake for smoko, and these old Aboriginal blokes never stopped going to the toilet for a helluva long time, because of the Epsom salts, see. They were all sitting in the swag and then one day one old Aboriginal fella goes over to Tommy and said, 'Tommy, I got a tummy-ache. You got any medicine?'

Tommy Cody said, 'Yeah, I got some medicine here I'll give you,' and he picked up his cup and put some Epsom salts in with some water. He said, 'Here, drink that. That will fix you up.' The old Aboriginal bloke looked at him. 'Go on, drink it,' he said. So he did, and as soon as he drank it he never stopped shitting again.

Then one day one old Aboriginal bloke walks up in the morning. 'Tom,' he said, 'I got a belly-ache.'

Tommy Cody says, 'I'll give you a belly-ache, just wait there.'

He was cooking away and he had a shovel in his hand for covering the bread up in a camp oven, and Tommy Cody picks up a shovelful of coal and spreads it all over this old Aboriginal bloke. This old Aboriginal bloke took off half-cooked and you could smell him for miles. 'We'll tell the manager on you,' they said, and they goes up and tells the manager about how he scalded the old Aboriginal bloke with the coals.

The manager jumped on his buggy and he goes and he sees old Tommy Cody. Tommy said, 'I couldn't give a damn if all Aboriginal people do get cooked, because they no use, they just hopeless.'

The manager says to him, 'They're not hopeless, they're useful because they're working for nothing, not like you and I. You're working for a pound a week. Those boys work just for shirt and trousers and a bit of tucker and they do a helluva lot of work.'

Then one of these Aboriginal blokes walked up to him and said, 'Tommy, what for you want to chuck a shovelful of coal over a man's head to get rid of him? You like mucking around with all our black girls too. You don't like the man, only the girls.'

Old Tommy Cody looks at him and he said, 'Well, I like the both of you. I like the black girl same as the black man.'

Anyway, gradually Aboriginal people woke up to old Tommy Cody with the Epsom salts and in the Aboriginal way they sang him, they sang his turd.

What happened was old Harry Huddleston saw him go down for a toilet, and when Tommy left they went across and picked up his turd and put it on a little leaf, and put it in a hollow log with some dry grass. They put a fire into the dry grass and sealed up the ends of the log so big lots'a smoke were trapped inside the hollow log, going around in circles. Then they sang that turd with a sacred song, and because the spirit from the song got mixed up with the smoke going around in circles, the spirit went into his turd and it went into old Tommy Cody's system, twisting him up to make him go crook. That's the way Aboriginal people do it.

Then old Knock-'em-Down-Tommy had the runs, and he said to me one day, 'Could you go 'round and get me some arsehole joy? Might cure my belly-ache.' He couldn't stop shitting, see, and the arsehole joy it's a little tiny fruit in the bush, *marna murran* is the name for it. He's very good food for belly-ache.

I said, 'All right,' and I went and brought this arsehole joy over to him and he drank some and that didn't make any difference to him at all—for him it wouldn't work because he's been sung, see. Anyway, he continued on and he was scouring a lot and then he got worse and he ended up going into town and went to hospital for a check-up. It took about a week all together from when they sang his turd till he died. He didn't know at all, otherwise he would have shot the bloke that sang it.

Then one day an old bloke called Oscar Edmondson came to talk to me. He was an old Norwegian bloke, he was a stock-camp cook, and they called him 'Hit Man' because he used to head-butt the other blokes. He talked to me about coming into the European camp. He said, 'You come this way and you live white man way. You get better clothing, you get a bit of money for yourself, and you get a good experience off the white man side. You learn a lot,' he said, 'I'll look after you.'

So I was brought in from the Aboriginal camp to be with the European, and first up I was very quiet you know. I never talked much. Because old Oscar was a Norwegian I couldn't understand him much, but he was a nice old cook, and he always looked after me there and he used to explain to me, 'The longer you stay in the European camp, the better you'll be. You might come a businessman maybe and know how to make a lot of money for yourself, and get a name for yourself, and you won't look back.' That's what he said, old Oscar, and he was looking after me.

Sometimes at night I'd run back down to the Aboriginal camp and have a yarn with my old mother Ludi, and then I'd go back to the white's camp to sleep, and there was a Scotsman there, old Peter Hogg, and he come around and talked to me. He said, 'I'll learn you how to read and write.'

'Oh,' I said, 'all right,' and the next thing he picked up the fruit tin label and tomato sauce label and he started teaching me how to read and write. He taught me how to sign my name, and the ABCs. I never forgot him. He was called 'Peter Crow' too—we used to say, 'Peter Crow comin',' because he had a big white eye on him, a blue spot, and a white ring around it like a crow. We never had a pencil, so of course we used charcoal for writing the letters, and I picked it up from him. Not really good schooling but good enough for me to understand. I can read 'Katherine' and 'Victoria River Downs', and things like that.

Then in 1950 old Peter Crow was gone, and there was no school at Willeroo, and I was more interested in learning about the bush way, the university under the stars, and when we got older we were really out in the field chasing cattle. Ten kilometres we'd be going out, heading north, mustering cattle, watching him in the pitch dark night without a moon when it's pouring rain and lightning flashing and bog everywhere. We were splashing in mud all around the country, and we still carried on watching cattle. We had four men watching at a time—first lot for two hours and after two hours another four will take over, all the way through the night, just riding around and around them, singing and talking to keep them quiet. The Aboriginal always sang Aboriginal songs, and European, he sang his song, and the cattle would listen to you sing and you'd put them to sleep. The cattle loved it, to hear us singing in the Aboriginal way:

> Walanga walanga dindin nya dindin nya
> Walanga walanga dindin nya dindin nya
> Walanga walanga dindin nya dindin nya
> Walanga walanga dindin nya dindin nya

That's what I would sing for the cattle, a Dreamtime song to keep them quiet. We sing it to the kids. It just says, listen, and lay down and go to sleep, like a lullaby.

And as we were travelling we were eating the bush tucker— the green plum, white berries, and we had black plums. I'll tell you, the Aboriginal was a very healthy Aborigine. As soon as we were born and growing up we were living on the bush tucker. It's got bush medicine in him, and you eat as you travel.

But now today the Aborigine are soft because they're living off pies and anything from the shop, very light stuff, and of course the booze on top of that. They're really weak, they lose a lot of teeth, but in early days you wouldn't see an Aboriginal with a toothache at all, because they lived on the bush tucker. We had wild banana, we had wild grapes, we had echidna, and we had kangaroos, and there's a goanna, and we had bush turkey. Oh, we had all sorts of tucker, and out in the stock camp if we had a European or an Aboriginal cook he always did curry and rice, or oxtail stew. I gotta have that meat and damper. I can't just live on potato, onion, and lettuce, and stuff like that. Sometimes in the camp it was just corned beef and damper all the way— never any potato or pumpkin or anything like this. Only when the property grew potato and pumpkin, then we had a supply from the homestead.

SCALE OF RATIONS FOR THREE MONTHS

ENDED 30th DEC. 1950

DECEMBER

ADULT RATIONS

> *28 lbs flour @ 4d.*
> *4 lb sugar @ 6d.*
> *12 oz tea @ 21/2 d.*
> *Baking powder*
> *2 tins treacle @ 1/-*
> *4 lb rice @ 7/-*
> *56 lb beef @ 4/-*

ISSUE—MALE ADULT

> *16 oz Nailrod tobacco @ 83/4 d.*
> *4 pcs soap @ 6d*
> *4 bxs matches @ 13/4 d.*

> *MANBULLOO STATION*
> *Tom Fisher*
> *A/c Willeroo & Manbulloo Ltd*

Then of course when we brought the cattle in from the stock camp we were taught to take the cattle into the big yard at the homestead and to do the inoculation—the dip. My mother used to do that work, carting the water with a 4-gallon drum on each side, filling the dip. They had already dug a big hole with pick and shovel and dynamite—it'd be 4 foot across, and about a 100 foot long, and as you are going in it's 3 feet deep, then 5, 10 and on to 20 foot, then 15 again, then 5, 2, 3, 1 right up to on top, they walk out then—he's on a slope, see. When I was a kid, before I started operating in the stock camp, I used to always carry a small billy can and follow my mum and put the water in the big dip. That used to take from morning till sunset, and then we put phenol in the water to kill the ticks, and then up to twelve or thirteen hundred bullocks got to swim in the dip, the whole big mob, all in a line.

Then we had twelve to fifteen hundred bullocks mustered from the bush, all clean, then a drover always turned up with a heap of Condamine bells on the horses, ting-a-ling-ing away and the whip cracking—you could hear them for miles. And you'd say, 'Here comes the drover, we gotta leave the cattle with the drover tomorrow.' That's when I was taught about counting the bullocks for the drover, and that's how I come to have my own business today. I started off from counting the bullocks, and I never looked back. It was old Harry Huddleston, my brother-in-law's brother, who taught the army to throw the boomerang who taught me how to do a headcount on the bullocks.

Often we had twelve to fifteen hundred bullocks come in from the bush after being mustered, and he'd be saying, 'One two three four five six seven eight,' and I followed Harry's mouth right up to a hundred and he'd put a knot in the whip. Then he'd go to a hundred again, and then put another knot in the end of the whip, all the way till we got up to about twelve hundred and fifty bullocks. Sometimes he used to count up to fifteen hundred and then when I was on my own I used to count in me own mind—I'd sit up there in me own self and count up to a hundred and then put the knot in the end of the whip, all the way to the fifteen hundred. 'Oh, that's the way it works,' I'd say.

Then the next time with the cattle for the drover a bloke called Rod McLennan was keeping the count and I'd be keeping count under my hat. The bullocks were galloping very fast and all bunched up together and we used to count up very fast. When the tail end of the cattle came through I said, 'Twelve hundred and fifty.'

He said to me, 'How'd you know?'

I said, 'I count them too.'

'Yeah,' he'd said, 'Oh jeez, you right. How'd ya do that?' I showed him the knot on the whip I had and he said, 'Oh Jesus, that's all right.'

Then after a while the cattle used to spread out a bit and I'll count them in threes and fives and eights and tens and eighteens and twenty fives and thirties and another eight will come, thirty-eight, and two come down that be forty—just like this all the way, see—and by the time we bunched them up together I'd go over to this drover and say, 'We've got fifteen hundred there.'

He'd say, 'How'd you know?'

'I just counted them.'

He'd look at me and he'd say, 'How'd you count them? Did you count them going down the water?'

I'd say, 'No, just now.'

'What? When they spread out?'

I said, 'Yeah.'

'Oh well, let's see.' And we'd go put them together and string them out and count them up. 'By Jesus!' he said, 'you right. Jesus, you must have a very good mind and very sharp eye.'

From there on I'd taken it up to be a good counter, and gradually I ended up getting five bob a week, and I was working out the penny and five pence and two pence, and the shilling. My first pay was about £16, and I bought some good gaberdine trousers, Williams boots, and hats and leggings and spurs. You couldn't do that today—that's $33, but today you'd have to pay about five hundred dollars, and you can't get gaberdine trousers anyway. They're finished.

Anyway, that was the start of how I come to have a good business today, first with the fencing, and now the tourism and the painting. When a job was ready I was on the ball. They always classed me as a very good man and I was happy. When I was in the Aboriginal camp I learnt a lot of the Aboriginal way, and when I was in the European camp I learnt a lot of European way, therefore now today I'm going both ways.

Chapter Fifteen

THANK YOU, OLD MAN

First I was a qualified stockman, and then in 1950 I become a mailman, bringing the mail in every wet season with the packhorse run from Willeroo to Manbulloo. I was getting five bob a week. Sometimes we did the run right to Delamere, but not always, and some others used to come over from Victoria River Downs to pick up their mail at Willeroo. Another mailman was coming from the depot at Timber Creek—it came there by boat—and they did another run to VRD and Wave Hill, and we did the mail run from this end at Katherine and connect with them for VRD.

Anyway, oh Jesus! In the Wet we used to ride along and hear the water running in the river in front of us, and we'd say, 'Oh, the river's up,' and unpack the packhorses and put all the pack bags in the tarpaulin and make a dinghy out of the tarpaulin, and swim the dinghy across and leave the gear on the banks of the river. Then swim back again and take the lead with one horse, and all the others will follow me into the river. When I get down to the middle water, I'll jump off my horse and float down on the western side of the stream. I always had a bunch of leaves in my hand and I'd start shaking these leaves and making lots of noise, and the horses would see me with the leaf moving and only my head sticking up, and they'd get a fright and they'd go faster and swim across quicker.

Then we'd pack them all up and take off again till you see another river, and you'd be doing the same thing every day. I was frightened of the rivers, but I was only a young fella and I could swim like a fish. We had about four or five rivers to swim over about 80 mile. That was a bugger of a game. King River was the hardest one. Limestone was a hardie if he was flooded. Scott Creek was another real hard one to cross. Mathison Creek was a really dangerous one— he had a lots 'a whirlpool in it. Then there was Bull Creek, which was very dangerous because it is narrow and runs very fast. All those rivers were very dangerous rivers, especially if you're unloading potatoes and bags of onions. That was a bugger of a thing on the mail run. Jesus! When those potatoes and onions were wet they were very heavy. All through the Wet we used to swim them rivers. Jeez it used to get monotonous. Today I'm driving past those rivers and I'm laughing at them because there's bitumen and a bridge over the top of them.

Before me, several Aborigine had been the mailman. The original mailman was old Dulu. Early in the piece lightning struck him and cut his hand off and he had hardly any hand at all. My old auntie Daisy, Joe Jomornji's sister, told me about this. She's still alive today, and when she was only a young girl they were walking around and old Dulu was chopping a tree to put up a grass tent, and the rain come along, and the lightning hits his tomahawk and took his hand off. This is the same as when we were kids, old Joe told us never to use the axe in the rain, or the lightning will hit you. Anyway, one fella, old Brinkin, was there—he was a granfa for me—and he raced over and he started singing him straight away. He said, 'Turn him over,' and he sang his full body, the lot, and they watched him start breathing, and he come back to life. They put him in the smoke then, and he was all right. They put the wild onion on the big sore he had— it was dripping—and that cured him.

Anyway, old Dulu was a letter stick man, and he had a letter stick tied up in the end of the stick with a plastic bag on top to stop it from getting wet. When you camp overnight you just stand that stick up beside you, and you get up in the morning and you pick up your letter stick and away you go again. He'd walk all the way, 80 mile of it from Willeroo to Manbulloo. He'd take the letter stick and give it to the bosses, might have been Johnny Newmarsh or Mr Moray at Manbulloo, and they

look at the letter and they'd give him lots 'a mail in the bag.
Then he'll carry it all the 80 mile of it back again.

When I took over from old Dulu, I was mailman until
1953, when they pushed the Victoria Highway through. One
day we're riding up and we can hear a noise coming. I said to
this old boy who was with me, old Billy, 'Something making
a noise, must be a plane somewhere.' We'd never heard a plane
much, only now and again, but anyway, this day we can hear
this noise coming closer and closer, and we reckon it's a plane,
and then we reckon it's some car. He was getting closer and,
'Strong motor car this,' we reckon. Next thing we saw the
bulldozer pushing all the trees over.

We reckon, 'Jeez, what he's doing just knocking all the
tree over?' Anyway, we took all the mail to Manbulloo and on
the way back we caught up with the bulldozer driver again—he
was only doing about 4 or 5 mile a day—and he was heading
all the way to the Western Australian border making the Victoria Highway. That's when the packhorse stopped, and I finished up as the mailman.

District Superintendent   26th February 1953
Native Affairs Branch
Darwin

REPORT ON MANBULLOO STATION

The only half-castes on the property are Billy Harney and Harry
Huddleston. The latter is well past middle age, is exempted and
is recognised as a competent stockman and useful station hand.
During 1952 he worked on Wave Hill and Delamere Stations
as well as Manbulloo. Billy Harney is under eighteen years, he
has a Commonwealth Savings Bank Book which when I saw it
last on the 13th of November, 1952, showed a credit balance of
£269.19.8. His wage as a youth stockman is £5.2.11. He is a
highly respected young man and capable at his work. It is a pity
that his knowledge of reading and writing is negligible. This
handicap will probably prevent him rising much higher than a
head stockman. He lives and eats with the white employees in
the stockman's quarters.

From 'Report on Manbulloo Station', by Patrol Officer J.R. Ryan

Then I became a saddler. This old bloke Alec Pott taught me

how to do the saddles in 1953 at Manbulloo, when I was with old Jerry Wren and Mrs Wren. They were taking good care of me because they knew that I had a lot of pull and I could become a good man. They called Alec old 'Teapot' because, oh Christ! he will drink tea by the bucketful, and he said, 'Here's the leather, here's the cotton, here's the wax. Roll the hemp on your leg like this.' He showed me how he did it and when I did it exactly the same he gave me the cotton, awl, and needle and the clamp. He said, 'This is the clamp so you can stitch the leather. If you gunna do the pack saddle, you gotta put the straw underneath and the horse hair on top of that, and quilt the saddle-church after.' The saddle-church is the cloth used for the bottom of a saddle, the surface that sits on the horse. Well with old Alec Pott, all of a sudden I can build a saddle, make a sandshoe and leather shoes, and then the plaited whip, or Anderson whip and a plaited belt. I could do a belt with four and five ridges because I used to always muck around with the bullock hide, and I made a lot of bullock hide belts and whips. Also, we used to make hobble straps to hang on the horses, and we used to plait out the neck strap to put around the horse's neck, all fancy looking you know, to make it look flash. And I always did that and they always passed my job.

Then I did the windmills. Old Norm Olsen was the only windmill expert around the country. He was a funny old fella. 'Snuffler Norman' we called him because he always talked through his nose and it sounded like a mosquito roaring inside a tank, and he used to go around and put the windmills up to pump the water. He taught me to climb up a tower and rig up all these fans, and how to put the rod down into the bore hole, and so I became the windmill man too. Of course now these days they've done away with the windmill—they got all these solar things to pump the water, just automatic electricity connected off the sun. Anyway, I learnt about putting up a windmill, and that was when I heard the story about old Jack Kilfoyle from over Rosewood Station, how in the dry season, he got short of windmills.

Old Kilfoyle was a wonderful man around the Rosewood area. One boy from Newry had an accident one time, and he broke his neck and he died, and Kilfoyle just said, 'Oh just bury him.' And another bloke was yarding the cattle and a big bullock hit him and broke his neck, and he died in the yard at Kinevan. Well Kilfoyle always used to say, 'Oh dear dear dear'—'Oh Dear Dear Kilfoyle' we called him—and when this second boy died he said, 'Oh dear dear dear, we lose a lot of men,' but he wasn't worrying about the men. He just said, 'Bury him here, and we'll get on with the work.'

He always used to ride around with binoculars over his shoulder and one day he was mustering and he saw one old boy in the binoculars, and this old boy was riding a cow. Kilfoyle turned around and he said, 'Oh dear dear dear, that cow was put there to get a nice herd, I don't want to see a human being gettin' on an old cow!' Jesus there was a laugh at that. Kilfoyle went over and shot the cow and he said to this boy, 'Oh dear, never do that again, gettin' on to my good cow.' And he said, 'I'm putting a good stud bull onto it, not you, you two-legged one. I want a four-legged one.' Jeez we laughed at that.

Anyway Norm Olsen was telling me, and when I was over at Gordon Downs in 1954 the old cook was telling me how the policeman arrested old Kilfoyle over the windmills. Gerard Beattie was telling me too—he was the brother of Linda, the first wife from my old man Bill Harney. In the whitefella way he was cousin to me, but in the Aboriginal way we were brothers. He worked for old Jack Kilfoyle for a long time, and he was sitting up and telling me that the dry season came along and Kilfoyle was short of windmills, and he goes over to old Farquarson's place down Inverway. He took a bottle of rum, and when old Farquarson was getting stuck into the rum at the homestead, old Kilfoyle had a bloke up the paddock pulling a couple of windmills down and loading them up and carting all these windmills from Inverway up to Rosewood—it's a fair way, 50 or 60 miles across country, I suppose—and they put it up and painted it, and it was pumping.

Then one day Farquarson went out to have a look at a bore and there was no windmill. Everything was gone—the legs and everything. He thought, 'Gawd almighty. What's going on? Who took the windmill? How the hell did it get away?' and he thought of Kilfoyle. They knew he was the greatest thief in the country. He'd thieve anything—cattle and horses, anything.

Anyway, Farquarson followed the track all the way right up to Rosewood, and old Kilfoyle was sitting over there at Rosewood and he hid the windmills in the grass. Anyway when he got to Rosewood, Farquarson seen old Kilfoyle and said, 'I tracked you all the way up here, and can I have a look around for my windmill?'

Kilfoyle, 'I wouldn't do a thing like that,' and anyway they put the cops on to him. The Northern Territory coppers come down, old Gordon Stott rode over there with the buggy from Timber Creek and he wanted to get the old Kilfoyle. But the Rosewood homestead was in Western Australia and the yard was built in the Northern Territory. The policemen were singing out to him from the Northern Territory side but they couldn't get him because he was on the WA side.

The police were saying, 'We just lookin' for a windmill. You haven't seen anybody take off with a windmill 'round this way?'

Kilfoyle says, 'No no no, dear dear dear, someone gotta be crazy to take that off. So heavy! How you gunna take that off in a hurry? God, got to be a lunatic to do that!'

Kilfoyle was sitting back on the Western Australian side laughing at them, so the Territory police go back and ring up the cops from Western Australia. They say, 'He's over the West side, could you get him and question him for the windmill?'

The Western Australia police go over, and they couldn't arrest him because he was on the Northern Territory side, and every time the Territory police came he went back to the West Australia side. They recognised the windmill under the paint, but they still couldn't get old Kilfoyle because he was across the border in Western Australia. Well what they did, the yard was on the Territory side and the police let all Kilfoyle's cattle out of the yard, and Kilfoyle races over to stop the cattle running off, and the cops came up behind and nabbed him.

Then again, old Gerard Beattie was telling me another story—that the coppers wanted some lunch, and they said, 'We gotta go down and get some tomato from the garden.' The garden was on the Territory side, and the coppers go to get the vegetables, and old Kilfoyle was walking down the garden to picking a watermelon, and the policeman followed him and said, 'I'm arresting you. You are over here on the Territory side.'

'Oh dear dear dear, you couldn't do that, we gotta have lunch.' So they arrested old Kilfoyle and took him down to Timber Creek, and had a yarn with him and took him to the court about this windmill.

In the mean time old Farquarson pops up and he says, 'Where's that windmill? I want it back.' Anyway, he gives him the windmill back and then the next thing they had a big fight over the windmill and Kilfoyle got fined $100, or something like that in those times.

Old Kilfoyle he had good property there and many good cattle on the property. He had a very quiet area and he thieved all the cattle off old Farquarson at Inverway, and he thieved some off old Durack, and he built his place up with the cattle from thieving because he was very Ned Kelly, old Kilfoyle. But with these new big companies taking over now, and chasing the cattle with the helicopters, and the cattle today is very wild, if old Kilfoyle had a look today he'd be surprised. He'll get a shock. It's not quiet any more. If he saw the country he'll go deeper into the graveyard, and say, 'Oh dear dear dear.'

Anyway, after the windmills I learnt well-sinking. First I used to watch old Harry Webb, the one who put down the well at Delamere in 1946. We were only kids but we used to always get down the bottom of the well to see what he looked like, and of course we got a little bit scared because that was a 40-foot well. He had two forked sticks beside the top, and a two-handled rail across the top and a big cable wire, and he'd spin the handle around and load the buckets with water and bring the bucket up—that's the way we always did it in the old time way.

Later I put in a lot of wells because I was with Bert Batty, and he did one well over at Killarney and I give him a hand to put the well down. And in 1959 I was with the old Aboriginal Jack Farquarson—son of old Harry Farquarson who used to be at Inverway—and he was a great well-sinker. He put many wells down Willeroo, and he always had his timber all the way down, and I was taught to put the well from old Jack. Now again the new way come in—this new type with the diesel motor. They just run automatically now, and they got one with the electric motor that works off solar—that's a new type again.

Anyway, I learnt all these things, and was still in the stock camp, and gradually when I was grown up I become what they call a supervisor—I was the head stockman—and I was head stockman for Vestey for 20 years. The supervisor's got the care of everything. He's the head of the camp. You make sure everything goes right. If you mustering, you got to make sure you get the amount of bullocks that the company asks for. If you didn't get that right amount of bullocks then people got the sack over it.

But with me, I had the ability for those sort of things. I had the push in me, plenty brains, hard worker, and from my experience from working I fit Aborigine into my work. They were my relations, but I was in charge and they worked in with me because I was a man with a lot of pull in me, and I wasn't slack. Even some of the blokes in my family, the older people, they reared me up, they taught me, and they were working with me too. I didn't go crook at them or anything like this. I more or less did their job too. I did everything, I was four men all in one.

And old Clarrie Wilkinson, the old fella from Willeroo who helped grow me up, I knew old Clarrie all his life, ever since I was a kid right up till he died in 1955. I was a full-grown young man then, and I was supervisor over at Flora Valley, and he came up and saw me. He said to me, 'Well, I'm so pleased at what I done to you. I made a man, and a good man out of you. I'm very pleased to hear what you're doing now. I heard a lot of people talking about you, they said you're first class.'

I said, 'Thank you, old man.'

PART FOUR

WORKING MAN (1955–80)

Chapter Sixteen

CLEANING UP WILLEROO

When I became a supervisor in 1955 I was still at Willeroo, and we shifted forty thousand head of cattle off Willeroo because the government was taking the land from Vesteys. See, they didn't equip their country with fences or a good yard, or good facilities for the Aborigine—they was just living on the place in a humpy—so the government came along and said, 'There isn't any improvement on the country, we gotta take the land off you,' and Vesteys lost Willeroo. At the same time they lost Gordon Downs, Birrindudu, Delamere and Margaret Station.

Then, just when the government was about to take the land off them, John Vestey and Edmund Vestey—they were the nephews for Lord Vestey—they come across from England. They wanted to see what the country looked like and they checked around all over, and they just kept the best of the stations. They said, 'We'll keep Wave Hill, we'll keep Helen Springs, and the rest can go,' and they got rid of the lot.

I met them when they come over. They're pommy. They were quite nice people, nice to talk to, and when they talked to us they said, 'You're great, great men!' They thought well of us because we did a lot of good turns for them—picking up lots of cattle and putting them in the markets—and they were getting a big heap of money for it. I was only getting five bob a week and they made heaps of money and never paid any tax, and they got away with it.

Over the period 1937–52, income derived directly from primary production in the Northern Territory by a resident of the Northern Territory was not subject to tax. The word 'resident' was not specifically defined, and through this loophole Vesteys

successfully appealed to the High Court against the Taxation
Commissioner's assessment in respect to income tax of one of
its properties. Because of the precedent established by the appeal,
'all of the non-resident pastoral companies shared in the con-
cession of freedom of income tax for fifteen years'.

From Peter d'Abbs, *The Vesteys Story*,
Australian Meat Industry Employees' Union, Victorian Branch, 1970

But later, when the tax man swung around and started chasing
them, of course they bolted, they left Australia, and I had to
supervise the big cattle round-up.

Well we shifted forty thousand head of cattle off Willeroo,
and then in 1955 I went to Birrindudu to clean up the last lot
of cattle in Birrindudu for Vesteys again. I went across on the
flight with Conair and when I got down there a manager bloke
called Stan Jones come along and met me at the airport and
took me out to the station, and I fitted in well with the Aborigines over there. I was working with them, not taking over
or anything like that—that way you get on well with the Aborigine, also with the manager. And every year I come back and
I visit my old mum, and she was very pleased to see me turn
up. And when the ceremony was on and I came back they'd
say to me, 'Here boomerang, run this song.'

I'd say, 'All right,' and I'd pick up a boomerang and start
straight away and sing the ceremony song for them. Then I'd
hang around Katherine there, and then go back for another
year, and we delivered the cattle to the drover.

Sometimes I went across to Wiluna in Western Australia to
give the drover a hand, and that's where there's amazing sand
ridges, sandhills as far as you can see, with a big wave on them,
and you go over one and down another, up another one and
down, and you go up another one and down, and we were riding
with the horses one day and I'm looking at this tree, but it's staying
in the one spot, not coming any closer. I couldn't work it out, but
then I saw that I'm just walking on the one spot—the horse is
walking but he's sliding backwards—and I'm looking at this tree
and it's in the same spot. I thought I was seeing things.

And I saw lots of Aborigines walking around in that

country, still on the move in 1956, the traditional way, naked. They lived the bush way all the time, and you couldn't talk to them because they speak different languages. You couldn't even put a rake through his head because they had fat in their hair— it was just all standing up like a lot of little wires, never seen a comb in their life—and a great big beard, strip bollocky naked, no clothes, women and all. But I heard that soon after I was there they moved across to Balgo Mission. Father McGuire was over there at Balgo Mission—that's south of Halls Creek—and he was coaching them in.

Then I come back from Birrindudu just when the government was about to take the land off Vesteys, to see how my mother was, and I had never been down south before, but I had a friend with me, a little white bloke called Tiny Derum, and I went with him to Townsville. He was in the army but he was running away, and as soon as we got there to Townsville they knew he was running and grabbed him. I was a bit worried when he went away, and I went over in front of the headquarters for the army, and I went in and seen the officer there. I said, 'My friend come in here. Am I allowed to go with him, to come in and get a job in the army?'

The colonel or someone was in there and they asked what I was, and I told them I was a ringer, a stockman, and all this, and they said, 'No we can't have a ringer.'

I said, 'Oh all right.'

Anyway, I jumped on the train from Townsville to Mt Isa, the old steam train, and a lot of those hobo drunks were along the road, drinking rum and everything with a party carrying on, and they kicked the toilet door open. Everyone was drunk, and the conductor come around to have a look to see what was going on, guitar going, yodelling away and everything, and I was sitting there just listening to it all. Anyway, I got over to Cloncurry and then I come into Mt Isa and I stopped there a couple of days. Then I jumped on a bus to Tennant Creek and come back home to Katherine, and I rang up the manager at Manbulloo and he said, 'I need you up here to do the final clean-up at Willeroo.'

I said, 'Oh all right,' and I went over to Willeroo and I did the final clean-up in early '57 to September '57. I was the last one at Willeroo to clean the last straggler that was left in the country. Then the government moved a caretaker in there to take over Willeroo before they sold it to another man, and Vesteys was gone from Willeroo. But Lord Vestey wanted all the Aborigines from Willeroo to come to Manbulloo Station. See, Vesteys were still running Manbulloo.

But the government said, 'We'll give them rations to stay at Willeroo.'

Then Lord Vestey was saying, 'They're my men!' The Aborigines were quite happy to stay on at Willeroo because this was their country, Wardaman country, but Vesteys said, 'No. I want the whole lot of youse to come to Manbulloo because you've been with us here and we gotta take you.'

The Aborigine said, 'Well all right, we'll go down to Manbulloo because more work there.' There wasn't work for them at Willeroo with the new caretaker because there was no cattle left there, and so they just shifted them across to Manbulloo. There was a huge number of Aborigine at Manbulloo, must have been about a thousand still employed by Vesteys at that one property—that's only 9 mile out of Katherine town—and Vesteys employed the whole lot. They would supply them with the feed, but no wages. But after the season finished there at Manbulloo, Bryce Killen bought Willeroo and next all the Willeroo mob went back and settled at Willeroo. That was in 1959, and they were all working at Willeroo right up till 1968.

Anyway, at the end of '57 I went across to Waterloo, that was a Vesteys station again, and in '58 I cleaned up Waterloo. I stayed with Vesteys right up till 1958 and I left then because one old bloke called Bill Mackie wrote to me to ask me to take up a block of land back on the Fitzmaurice River, on the western side of Willeroo. He was just an old white bloke that had been mining all his life, and he was a friend of my father, old Bill Harney. That's how I got tangled up with him. Bill Mackie borrowed some money from Primary Producers in Darwin to buy all the horses and saddles and stuff like this, and I asked my dad to give me some money to help me to start off the property. He send me £100 first up, and then later he gave me another £300, and a pound note was big money that time.

I said, 'I'll give you it back when I get the money back.'

Anyway I was with Bill Mackie there and we didn't get on well together. I wanted to muster cattle, but old Bill Mackie said, 'No no, leave the cattle till last, we'll go gold hunting.' Gold wasn't suitable for me because I was a cattleman, and so I ended up leaving him there at the end of '58—he still has money owing to me—and that's when I come in and worked with old poddy-dodging Tex Moar, and this was the first time I was poddy-dodging, with old Tex Moar the *wanga* man. As soon as old Tex got on the rum he'd pick up a tobacco tin and yodel his head off singing the Aboriginal song, the *wanga*, proper blackfella song. He'd take off his clothes and he could sing for hours, and he'd pull out a pocket-knife from his belt and make out, gammon way, with the kids there that he was going to cut their foreskin off.

Tex was missing one toe, too. How this happened, he was on the turps one time, and he was somewhere out in the bush because the police was after him for something or another, might be poddy-dodging, and he was on the grog and he went to sleep with his boots by his side. Anyway, he had a revolver there beside him, and old Tex is sleeping away on his back in the bush, and when he wakes up he's squinting out of his eye, and after all the grog what he can see is someone looking at him from over in the bush—but all he can really see is his big toe sticking up! But old Tex thinks this big toe is the policeman, and he slowly reaches over for his revolver, and he aims at his big toe, and bang! he shoots his big toe right off!

Anyway, Tex was one of the greatest poddy-dodgers round this area. Old Tex poddy-dodged many cattle in his time. Everywhere he used to muster. He used to hang back all through the winter till the wet season come, and when every other station closed down he'd start. He used to go around and thieve the horses and cattle, luring it back to hide it away in some nice big pockets on his property around Dorisvale, and then he'd go back and get another load.

Tex Moar knew that Willeroo country was vacant—only the caretaker was there before the Killen brothers took over in about January 1959—and Tex Moar said to me, 'Oh you've been working on Willeroo all your life, you'd be the ideal bloke to do a bit of dodging around Willeroo.'

I said, 'Yeah all right, I'll be in it,' and I was with him then.

See, the stragglers we left behind in the Vesteys clean-up were breeding quick, and away we went exploring around the country, and the rain was pouring, and we were mustering cattle in the night, all over Willeroo. It was just government land then, and everyone was raiding the country out, and so we got quite a few cattle for the Hong Kong market. We used to swim the floodwater all through the rainy night with the monsoon rain. He worked really hard, did old Tex. We were swimming across the Ferguson River in between Florina and Claravale, and there was a lot of man-eating crocodiles, and a few cattle was taken by them, and we were pretty scared to swim with a mob of cattle. Anyway we got the cattle all the way to Katherine. We got eleven hundred total, all cleanskins, unbranded, and I got £10 a week, and we come into Katherine and loaded the cattle to Hong Kong—that was in February '59, and that was my first time poddy-dodging. But I knew all the old time poddy-dodgers from when I was a boy—they were all like Ned Kelly—and one of the biggest was old Wason Byers, and this is the story of Wason Byers.

Chapter Seventeen

HE HAD NO FRIENDS

I knew old Wason Byers first in 1942, but first I'll tell you what's been happening before, with old Wason Byers around Wave Hill.

There was this young Aborigine boy down there at Wave Hill, he was a bastard to play the didgeridoo—he never stopped and everyone kept on knocking off his didgeridoo, and he'd always race down and get it again and was always playing the thing. After a while I think the didgeridoo got on old Byers' nerves and old Byers gets up. 'Come over, boys,' he said. Everyone come down. 'I'll give some tobacco to the boy who always plays that didgeridoo. Put your hand up.'

Of course the young fella put his hand up straight away. His name was Tommy Dodd, he was a Gurindji man. 'Oh, you the bloke that play the didgeridoo? All right, come over,' old Byers said, 'here's the tobacco.' And he give him a bit of tobacco. 'Sit down,' he said, 'I want you to pick up the didgeridoo.' The boy goes across, picks up his didgeridoo and brings it down. Byers plonked his swag down there and lay down. 'All right,' he said, 'you play the didgeridoo for me.'

The boy played the didgeridoo and he was blowing and blowing and blowing and blowing and blowing, and then the boy turned around and said, 'That's all boss, my mouth's getting a little bit sore.'

'Oh no, that's really good music, boy,' he said. 'Keep on blowing. I'll give you more tobacco later on, keep on blowing.'

He continued on blowing and blowing and blowing and his mouth was going bigger. 'I got a sore mouth, boss.'

'Blow, you bastard, blow,' old Byers said. 'You been blowing it for the last week,' he said, 'keep on blowing, keep on.' Anyway he blowed right up till sunset, and every time the boy stopped blowing Byers fired a shot next to him with the revolver. 'Now blow it, go on, hurry up, if you run away, I'm gunna blow your leg off.' He had him frightened, and the boy ended up blowing till his mouth was like a big blister, oh Jesus! like a big balloon—just like if you have an apple on your mouth.

'Now,' Byers said, 'that ought to fix you up. You won't blow a didgeridoo any more.' The boy couldn't hardly even lift up his lip in the end. Byers said, 'Whenever you blowing didgeridoo, I'll have you blowing again,' and that settled the boy down.

Then later, after he finished up at Wave Hill, Byers went across to Sturt Creek, just on the Western Australian border, managing the property for Vesteys again. When he was down there a lot of old Aborigines spoke about old Byers. They said, 'Oh he was a good old boss, old Wason Byers, but again, on the other end, he was a bastard. He was a hard man, you know, always flog Christ out of us with the whip'.

One old man called Lightning was telling me that one day he was down there, and some Aboriginal ladies were digging up the garden and one of the ladies stole another one's billy can—they used to always water the garden with the billy, see. They were called Winnie and Elsie, and one lady couldn't find her billy, and she said, 'Oh you got my billy? I want my billy back.'

This other lady said, 'No, you got your own billy and we gotta have it separate.'

The next thing they put on a turn and the two were fighting. They fought and fought and everybody was shouting, and old Byers got up and looked over to see what was going on, and everybody tried to stop them, and next old Byers gets up and walked out of the house and he said, 'Come here, you girls.'

Both of them went over and old Byers was standing up there and he said, 'I'll put this 44-gallon drum up here, I want you two girls to go up on top of the roof.'

They said, 'No, I can't.' This is around about October and you could see the heat dancing on the tin roof.

Byers said, 'Yes, go on!' and he pulled a revolver and flogged them with the whip. He said, 'Take your clothes off!' They took their clothes off, and he said, 'Now, get up that roof there!' and he stood up there with a revolver and these two girls got up and he made them sit down on the roof.

They couldn't sit down at first because the tin was very hot, and he's standing up on the 44-gallon drum with a fork stick and he dug the fork stick in their flank and around the rib and he made them sit down, and they were sitting down and walking around, jumping around, their feet was getting hot, their arse was getting hot and oh, he was doing all sorts of things to make them sit down. He fired a shot up in the air, and they were sitting down and screaming, and then he made them move over to another hot place and he had them for about a quarter of an hour, sitting down in this hot heat. Then he made them come down. 'Now put your clothes on,' he said, 'now!'

He took them inside into the dining room. He grabbed their two head together, 'Now,' he said, 'I'll give youse fighting! If you want to fight you two can have a fight here,' and he grabbed the two heads, one on each hand, and he bashed their heads together, head to head. He said, 'Now that's teaching you, no more fighting. I don't want to hear any more fighting in the camp. If you do that,' he said, 'I'll be putting you in the charcoal in the hot fire.'

They said, 'Yes, yes,' and the Aboriginal lady was terrified.

When they went back to the camp there was not a sole Aborigine left in the camp—they had cleared bush. They were heading across to Gordon Downs, and on the way down they met Clarrie Wilkinson, and old Clarrie was telling me that he seen this string of Aborigines all walking up and he said, 'What's going on with you mob? You on a holiday?'

'No,' they said, 'that Wason Byers he too hard. He make everybody take clothes off, put 'em up on top of the iron and he's there with the revolver and poking them and belting everyone up, and all this sort of thing, you know. Look at that two girl there.'

These two girl come over and said, 'Look at us, he put us on the top of the roof,' and they lift their dress up and showed their arse. Well they had the greatest blister Clarrie ever seen, just like big balloons, one on each cheek of the arse, poor bastards.

Clarrie Wilkinson swung his horses back and went home to Gordon Downs and with the pedal wireless he sent a telegram across to the Vesteys that Wason was too hard to the Aborigines. Anyway old Mr Moray the travelling boss come along and sacked old Byers because he was too cruel to the Aborigine.

That was round about 1943, and old Byers got the bullet and left there and he come into town and he started up droving, and he was driving a lot of cattle from the Western district over to the army abattoir at Manbulloo just out of Katherine. He was droving for a long while right up till 1948, and in 1949 when Coolibah Station come up for sale he went in and then he bought it. He was teed up with Tom Piper to go in and share with him, and they bought Coolibah and Bradshaw Station in 1949.

There was hardly any cattle left in the property because it'd been scooped out by old Tom Quilty—he was the fella that sold it to them—and he shifted all the cattle across from Coolibah and Bradshaw to Western Australia, where he went, and the place was very bare of cattle.

Tom Piper said to old Byers, 'There's hardly any cattle in the area. We spent a lot of money on this and we need lot of bullocks to pay for the property.'

'Oh,' said old Byers, 'there's about fifty thousand head in the area.'

Tom Piper said, 'Oh yeah?'

Old Byers reckoned, 'No worries, I'll make it pay.' But Byers was bullshitting because there was no fifty thousand there at all—there was flat out being five hundred head left in the country. Anyway Byers didn't do any stock musters all through the dry season, but he was poddy-dodging all the other places all through the wet season. He used to muster all the cattle off the other properties and he used to stock his paddocks up all through the Wet.

He raided Victoria River Downs every year from 1949 till 1953, and by the middle of March he'd be ringing up to call the drover to come down, and he used to send three thousand bullock every year off Coolibah to Ross River meatworks in Townsville—and they were all Victoria River Downs bullocks. Victoria River Downs had a bull's-head brand and Coolibah had MTQ brand, and all he done he just put a Q over the bull's-head to blotch the brand so you couldn't see the bull's-head.

And each year he always rang Victoria River Downs—Jimmy Martin was a overseer and Scott McColl was a manager—and he used to say, 'My drovers are going through Victoria River Downs to Queensland with three thousand head of bullock. If you want to inspect the bullock you can, but if you don't want to that's all right.'

'Oh that's okay, old Byers,' they'll say, 'we believe you.' See they were frightened of him, because they knew he was a dirty sort of a man.

Anyway, there's one track leading off to Camp Oven Bore, and I met old Wason Byers down there one time. He came down with a load of cattle, and it was the middle of the day and we had lunch there. After the lunch old Wason was just lying back on the ground, and he got one of the Aborigines that was working for him to boil the billy for a cup of tea. He was lying there and he called out, 'That billy boiled yet?'

This boy said, 'No.'

Wason Byers was still lying there, and after a while he called out, 'That billy boiling yet?'

The old boy said, 'Close up.'

Byers was still lying on the ground, and he calls out again, 'That fuckin' billy boiled yet?'

'Just about,' calls the boy.

Well Wason gets up and he shout, 'I'll give you "just about",' and he comes up and he kicks that billy up in the air like a football, and the billy water went over all these black-fellas, and old Byers says, 'Do it again, boil the bastard to pieces! Pile the wood onto it!'

So the next time these boys got lots of wood, and they piled it up on the fire, and the billy was in the middle and you couldn't see the billy for wood.

See the Aborigine always makes a small fire, but the white man makes a big fire, and this billy boiled in two minutes flat, and then old Wason had his cup of tea—we had it together. He had about two hundred bullocks there, and he saw me carrying a gun and he said, 'We've got a lumpy jawed bullock in there, a cancer one. Can you get rid of him?'

I said, 'Oh, I don't want to shoot your cattle.'

'Oh, he's right,' he said. 'You go in there and shoot him and you can inspect the cattle at the same time.'

Well I went in there and I rode right through them and we shot the old lumpy jawed bullock. And when I seen the stock they was nearly all Victoria River Downs bullocks he had. But I never said anything. He said to me, 'You got any complaining now?'

I said, 'No, old man.'

He said, 'You're a good little lad! I'll buy you a pair of boots and hat when I come back.'

I said, 'Okay,' and when he came back after he delivered all the hot bullocks into the butcher's, he brought me a hat and boots, and I was happy with that. He drove all that hot cattle right past people's noses, through Willeroo, and nobody would say anything to him because they were scared of him. Also, when he had driven through Victoria River Downs he'd meet old Jimmy Martin at the turn-off—old Jimmy Martin was the overseer and he was supposed to check all those cattle—and he'd say to Jimmy, 'Well, you could go in and have a look at the cattle there if you think there's any-thing wrong with them.'

Jimmy would say, 'Oh no, you ride away, seeing as we

know you. You're a good man. You can continue on with the cattle,' and that's how he carried on right through from 1949 till 1953, and old Tom Piper was pleased about how many bullocks a year was going to the Ross River meatworks—loads and loads of bullocks were going into the tin beef and old Tom Piper thought it all Coolibah bullocks. See, old Tom Piper, he knew nothing about what Byers was up to.

Then later I was at Willeroo working on the cattle and old Byers had an old boy called Kelly working for him, and old Kelly had two wives—one old wife and one young one—and of course these two ladies were jealous and would fight one another. When they fought there at Coolibah, old Byers stripped the lady there and flogged her with the whip and locked her in the storeroom, and old Kelly goes down to the house and was making an inquiry for his old missus. Old Kelly said, 'Where's my wife?'

Byers said, 'You got your wife over there.'

'No,' he said, 'that young one you got in there my wife.'

'She's not coming out because they fight too much, she's staying in the house,' and then Byers ended up getting the whip and flogging old Kelly with the whip.

Old Kelly turned around and said, 'All right, I'll fix you up.'

Well Kelly and Nancy Draper—that was Kelly's daughter—and their old mother, they headed across from Coolibah, they walked all the way right to Willeroo. When they got to Willeroo, old Kelly came and talked to me because he happened to be my uncle, and he was telling me about how old Wason Byers thieved cattle all the time, all through Victoria River Downs, through Willeroo country, and down to Auvergne side—all them places he's been mustering all through—and how he always put that Coolibah brand over another man's brand. And Kelly said, 'I'm putting him in.'

I said, 'Oh yeah?'

He said, 'Where's the manager?'

'Well,' I said, 'the manager he'll be there this afternoon.'

Anyway the manager Jerry Wren come and Kelly told the

manager about old Byers stealing all his cattle and the manager said to him, 'You telling the truth?'

That old Aboriginal bloke said, 'Yeah.'

He said, 'What make you think to dob old Byers in?'

'Well, I got another wife,' he said, 'and Wason Byers took her off me. He got him locked up in his store.' He said, 'He can't let him out. I'm gunna see Welfare. Welfare might help me to go out and get that girl out of the station and put old Byers in gaol.'

The manager said, 'Oh, you might be right. I'm gunna go down to Top Springs because there's a big manager meeting over there. I can tell Victoria River Downs manager what Byers been up to.' He said, 'The cattle that's leaving Coolibah now, they'll be going through there very shortly. They might stop 'em just to inspect the cattle, and see whether they Victoria River or Coolibah cattle.'

Anyway, Kelly came to Katherine and the manager of Manbulloo said to Ron Ryan from the Welfare, 'I'll leave the boy with you here. And about old Wason Byers locking the Aboriginal lady in the store,' he said to Ron Ryan, 'you can chase after that side, I'm gunna chase after old Byers for stealing all the Victoria River Downs cattle.'

Anyway, Jerry Wren goes over to Top Springs and they were all sitting down having a yarn and he brought this story up about old Wason Byers. But they didn't know that old Byers was doing it from 1949, and they went in and they called the manager, Scott McColl, and Scott McColl said to Jimmy Martin, 'I want you to go down and block those cattle over there at the border of our fence. Just go through 'em.'

Jimmy Martin raced up there and the first drover there in the front was Bill Sharpe and the second lot of drovers was Bill Ellis. That was cattle for Wason Byers that they were taking down, and Jimmy stopped them and just had a look around. They could see a couple of brands showing through underneath but they said, 'Oh you're right, you can come through.'

Anyway, the cattle continue on up to Pussycat and they had to put them through the dip, and a stock inspector come down to inspect the cattle and he said, 'Yes, there could be something false in those cattle all right, with the Coolibah brand on top of the old VRD brand.' See, when they put the cattle through the dip, the hide of the bullock was very wet, and then the little bull's-head brand from VRD showed through and they had a look at the whole lot of cattle and they said, 'We'll quarantine some of these cattle for about several months, just to see whether the new brand might die out and the old brand might show up.' Which it did, and the old brand did show up after a while.

Anyway, they continued on with a load of cattle right up to Anthonys Lagoon, and by that time they made the decision about arresting old Byers. They said, 'We gotta hang on to all the cattle over there and then charge old Byers, who's thieving the cattle off another man's property, you know he's the greatest cattle rustler.'

Old Byers was back at Coolibah, and there was another old Aboriginal bloke at Coolibah, old Hector—in Wardaman he was *Gulongarri*— and one day he looks over down the other side of the creek and he could see the cloud of dust coming, and it stopped, and this old boy walks down to have a look. These two old policemen were there on the creek, old Gordon Stott and Tas Fitzer—they were getting old and buggered— and old Hector sees these two old policeman getting into their uniform and talking about how to get Byers.

Hector come back and he said to old Byers, 'Hey old man, there's two policeman there down the river. I don't know what they doing in there.'

'Oh that's funny,' old Byers said, but he knew what they was after. He waited a bit and he said, 'Oh well, they're maybe gunna creep up on me with the gun or something.'

Anyway, he jumped on his little Chev ute and drove down to the river and he pulled up on top of the bank and he walked down and he spotted them and he yelled out, 'What are you doing in here, you pair of bastards!' He said, 'Don't be a blackfella sitting 'round the banks of the creek, come over to the house, I know what you after. You want to talk to me?

Come over to the house and talk to me, come over here.'

'Oh, we was gunna come down pretty shortly, we only filling up the radiator.'

'Oh, the radiator me arse!' he said, 'I know what you up to. Come over straight away!'

'Oh righto,' they said, and they followed him down to the house.

He had a pot of tea ready and he puts the chair down for himself and they squat on the floor. They looked at one another, old Gordon Stott and Tas Fitzer—they didn't know what to say. Anyway, old Byers said, 'I know what youse after. Spit it out!' he said, 'Straight away! No mucking round!'

'Oh well,' old Tas Fitzer said. 'Well, what we are up to . . . in the law . . . we are police . . . '

Byers said, 'Yes I know you're a police,' he said. 'Bring it out!'

'Well,' he said, 'you know we are police, we gotta do the job . . . what we was told over there . . . .'

Byers said, 'Yeah, yeah, carry on, I'm listening.' He was standing up with his two hands over the table, see.

They thought, 'The fuckin' old bastard's gunna hit us over the head with the chair or something.' Anyway, they said, 'About this cattle rustling, you know in Victoria River Downs district . . . they put a press on us to come down and do something with you, we gotta take you in to Anthonys Lagoon.'

'You will not take me!' he said. 'You take the lead and I will follow you!'

'Oh all right, Byers,' they said, 'all right. Yeah, you can come along behind us. Yes, yes, all right.'

'Anyway,' old Byers said, 'that I was stealing the cattle, well that's all crap!'

'All right,' and they had a quick cup of tea, and said, 'righto, let's go.'

They jumped on their police car, the old Land Rover, and he jumped on his little ute and followed them all the way into Katherine to the old police station, and old Sergeant Smythe was there, and old Sergeant Smythe said, 'How you going, Wason?' Dennis Smythe, he was a mongrel thing, see, and he said, 'Under the law we gunna put a charge on you for cattle rustling. You raided the Victoria River Downs district, I don't know for how long, but you up for stealing the cattle.'

'Good-oh, that's all right,' old Byers said, 'but I got something to tell youse later on.'

Then the Welfare bloke Ron Ryan come in with a summons for locking the old Aboriginal lady up and old Byers spotted him. He said, 'What are you after, you blackfella crawling bastard?' See Ron Ryan, he was on the Aboriginal side. 'Best you stay right out of it,' said Byers, 'otherwise, I'll wring your neck.'

Ron Ryan pulls up and then old Dennis Smythe the old cop walks around and said, 'We got him in gaol and then after a while you can come in with your case. But first we'll charge him with the cattle rustling,' and then old Ron Ryan stayed out of it.

Anyway, they charged old Byers for cattle thieving and after a while Tom Piper knew about it and of course old Tom Piper was jumping up and down and Byers goes over and tells Tom Piper, 'No need for you to jump up and down, keep your hat down.'

Old Byers, he brought old Mick Vandelour the lawyer from Innisfail in Queensland to defend him—he's a great lawyer—and Tom Piper said, 'Well, after this case, we'll have to just sell the property, we could call it square.'

Byers reckon, 'Yeah, that's okay,' and when they were waiting for the case Byers was putting three thousand hot bullocks to Queensland, he was putting about five hundred hot bullocks at a time over to the butchers in Darwin, and he made lots of money out of them.

Anyway, we were all sitting around down the stock camp one day at the back of Manbulloo in about October 1953, and the manager arrived from Manbulloo. 'Well,' he said, 'old Byers going up on this case tomorrow. We hope that fuckin' bastard go to gaol and get ten years and get hung. I like to see that, I laugh me fuckin' head off.' Well everybody was sending a cheerio to old Wason Byers, and good luck to him going to gaol, and everybody laughing about it—all over the Northern Territory they knew what a mongrel man he was.

Then his case was held over at Anthonys Lagoon. Gordon Stott was there, old Tas Fitzer was there, old Jack Mahoney the other policeman was there, old Dennis Smythe was there— oh, there was quite a lot of them there. They had a judge and they had all these Aborigines from Coolibah over there as a witness. They went along and old Byers had to sit down and listen, and they had this Aborigine Big Hector in the witness box. The policeman had already taught them that there was no need to be frightened, to tell what sort of a bastard of a man Byers was. The policeman had said to all the Aborigines, 'Just bring it all up, because we got him locked up, he can't do anything with you. You can do what you like. You can dob him in for everything you seen, put him in for the whole lot.'

That's what the police told all the blackfellas, and they all believed it then and they reckon, 'Yeah that's all right,' and first they put Big Hector in the courthouse.

'What's your name?'

'Hector Gulongarri.'

'How long you known Wason Byers?'

'Oh, I was born in Coolibah, and I belong to Coolibah and Wason Byers come along and he bought Coolibah.'

'What sort of a man is he?'

'Oh, him hard bugger. He was a mongrel man.'

'What do you call a hard bugger?'

'Well if we didn't do anything he told us to do he would flog us with a whip.'

'Oh, yeah, and what did he do after that?'

'Well he told us to catch a horse, put a saddle on, go out to Victoria River Downs.'

'Oh, yeah, and what you do over there at Victoria River Downs?'

'Byers say, "Bring the bullock, we want VRD bullock", and we try tell him, "Too many stranger bullocks, we can't bring him in because they stranger bullock for Victoria River Downs," and Byers say, "Bring all the Victoria bullock, we want them, because they're beef." '

Anyway, they got another boy, Barney, he was talking the same story. 'If you didn't bring the Victoria River Downs bullock,' they said to Barney, 'what would happen?'

'Well, Wason Byers said, "You gotta go back and bring a big lot of bullock, bring 'em in here," and we been bring one thousand bullock to yard here, and old Wason Byers always bring a handful of tobacco, lot of silver coin, and he said, "You good man, you very good boy." And anyway old Wason Byers said, "Put a brand on that one there, put this Q over that bull's-head, like this." That's what old Wason Byers tell us.'

'Oh yeah, and what was the Coolibah brand?'

'MTQ.'

'And what you put over that bull's-head?'

He said, 'Q over that bull's-head.'

'Oh yeah.'

'And we tried to tell Wason Byers not to put that MTQ brand over that bull's-head, because he was a stranger bullock. We frightened, that's what we told Wason Byers, and Wason Byers said, "You brand him, you black bastard, brand him or I'll flog you." Anyway, we went on and brand him. And any big brand that was in there, you know, one the little MTQ will not cover, he used to tell us, "Put a M brand over it," and we had to brand what he told us to. We been frightened of old Wason Byers. He'd stand over us walking 'round in the yard, backward and forward with a sharp stick. We didn't move, he'll poke us with the stick and make us work, you know, and that was old Wason Byers.'

'Oh yeah.'

Anyway, they move all the Aborigine out of the case, and they had old Byers in the witness box then, and old Byers said he owned Coolibah; he's been with Vesteys for quite a long while; he got into trouble with one of the Vesteys property for putting the Aboriginal lady on the roof, and he finished from there and he become a drover—he was a drover around in the

Katherine district; when he finished droving he started up a small property at Fitzroy; when he finished there he went across and bought a block of land at Coolibah Station, bought off Tom Quilty; and he was in share with Tom Piper.

'Now Mr Byers,' the judge reckons, 'you here today, being charged for the cattle rustling, for thieving all the cattle off Victoria River Downs district, few other places beside that, Auvergne Station, Willeroo, Delamere, some of the Vesteys property. Anyway, of course we gotta prove that's the Victoria River Downs brand in the bullock. We even shot some of them cows, see, and there's a hide there it's got MT bull's-head on it not MTQ—just a MT bull's-head—so there's the evidence showing in there.' Old Byers was sitting with his head down, see, listening to this and then the judge said, 'That's what you charged for.'

Then his lawyer old Mick Vandelour talked, he criss-crossed the ceremony, and said, 'You got an answer, Mr Byers?'

Byer stands up. 'Well,' he said, 'I owned the property at Coolibah. Aboriginal people,' he said, 'don't understand what you talking about in European language, they haven't been in a school. Well, I send the Aboriginal boy out in the field to muster the cattle, to bring the cattle into the yard. I told the boys to draft all the stranger out and I told them to brand all the Coolibah bullock. But they put cross brand over the strange bullock and I didn't know anything about it.' That's what he told them. 'I just heard it from you right now in the evidence there. If the Aboriginal did all this cross-branding, I was not knowing about it,' and that's the way he got off, just over that, because he said the Aborigine didn't understand the English. They cross-branded the bullocks themselves in the yard when Byer wasn't there—that's what he said—and that's when they dropped the case and he got off.

When he got out of it, the manager from Manbulloo told me, 'Byers, that old bastard out now.'

I said, 'Is he out?'

He said, 'Yeah, fucked if I know how he got out.' They said when he got out the policemen Gordon Stott and Tas

Fitzer kept old Byers in there for a bit till they get all the Aborigine cleared out, because when he walked out of the gaol he looked for them—he was gunna kill the bastards. He accused them for giving a false statement. He went down to the woodheap there at the back of the courthouse, he picked up a stick and started walking round looking for them. The old blackfellas all took off, past Coolibah and continued on to Kimberley, and they finished up at old Durack's place at Kildurk (Amanbidji), right up till old Byers died. They still over there some of them old boys, the ones that dobbed him in.

Anyway, I come to Katherine in 1960, and there's old Byers in Katherine. He was getting old then, see, and I'm sitting down and old Byers said, 'Where you now, young fella?'

I said, 'I'm down at Gordon Down.'

'Well,' he said, 'you remember the time that I met you along the road there in 1952 at Camp Oven Bore?'

I said, 'Yeah.'

'I was surprised,' he said. 'You were the only one person to see those stranger bullocks that I had in there coming across from Coolibah to Katherine district into the butchers over here. You knew those bullocks was there, but you never ever squealed on me.' He said, 'I'm gunna shout you a beer, young boy.'

I said, 'Oh, very good of you, Wason.'

He said, 'I like you young fella, you're a good lad.'

I said, 'Oh yes.'

'Only one small thing that I did wrong at Coolibah—locking up the wife for Kelly. He was the only one put me in. Otherwise I would have continued on at Coolibah. I could've come down and picked you up and took you over there to come a working boy for me, because I known your father for a long while, we always been a friend together.'

> Leaving Brunette [Downs] I travelled eastward, to camp at a curious lagoon called Connell's Lagoon . . . It was just a hole in the plain, as though a meteor had landed there in the past.
> At Connell's was an old droving mate of mine called Wason Byers, and he had over a thousand head of cattle with the Bull's

Head brand. As they grunted at night, to the chant of the natives on watch, I heard one of the white drovers on watch sing a bush ballad—It was known as 'The Combo's Anthem':

They are comely and dark, and the glint of their eyes
Are as dew-drops that gleam on a wintry sunrise.
And the firm rounded breasts that seductivly tease
Are like seed-pods that sway from squat boabab trees . . .
I smiled as I heard the song . . .

W.E. Harney, from Life among The Aborigines, Lansdowne Publishing, Sydney, 1995

Anyway, old Wason said to me, 'Old Bill never pass me, he always pull up and have a yarn, we always got on well.'

I said, 'Oh yeah.'

Of course I knew my old man old Bill Harney and Wason Byers always got on well—but I knew too that they hated one another in the back stabbing-way—face to face they were friends, but behind backs they were enemies. See someone might say to Wason Byers, 'Where is old Bill Harney?'

'Oh that bloody gin jockey bastard, he's over there somewhere cuddling the gin now. Little bugger,' he said, 'not worth feeding with the raw hide. He's sweet to the Aborigine, you know, talking to 'em and sitting in among them. He should have been one of the Aborigine.' That's what the old Byers would say.

Anyhow, when he come over to old Bill he'd say, 'How you going, Bill?'

'Oh all right, have a cup of tea'—they're mates again, see.

And if someone came along and asked Bill what happened to Byers, Bill would say, 'Oh that bloody whingeing bastard, he's over there. He hates bloody Aborigine. I don't know why, because the Aborigine got nothing to do with him. The Aborigine is a very nice boy,' he'd say, 'but old Byers hates them. He got no time for 'em, he likes to bloody kill 'em, and put the naked women up on top of the roof. That's cruel.' That's what old Bill would say.

Anyway, of course then Wason Byers arrives and old Bill would say, 'Oh, how you going, Wason. Come in and tie your horses and have a cup of tea.' That's what old Bill would say—

they were mates again, but they hated one another from a distance.

See everybody relied on everybody in this country, and that's why they had to be mates, including from European to Aborigine. The Aborigine made sure the European never got bushed, they were always out on the run to bring him in and look after him. Even if the white man hated Aborigine, the Aborigine still went to look for him and picked him up and looked after him.

Anyway, I always got on well with old Byers, and we had a beer there in Katherine, and he said, 'Well I won't be seeing you round this country any more.' He said, 'I'm gunna go down to Queensland while I'm old enough to be pensioned off.' He was about seventy-five then, I think, and not so long ago he died, in 1984, at Oban Station, and that was the end of Byers. Oh he wasn't a friend by black, white, yellow, man, women, human, dog and cat. He could shoot you before he ever look at you. He had no friends, and he was the biggest poddy-dodger of the lot.

Chapter Eighteen

THE METHO KING

After I was finished poddy-dodging with Tex Moar at Willeroo—that was in early 1959—I came across old Jack Davidson the drover, old Ingunn Ngunnin Davidson. That means he was very tall—6 foot 10 I think, 2 metres high, like a long whip—and he said, 'You like a job? I'm looking for some men.'

I said, 'What you do?'

'I gotta take a load of cattle to go from Humbert River to Wyndham.'

I said, 'Righto, I'll take a job on,' and I went with him on a plane over to Victoria River Downs, and I had to ride a horse across from Victoria River Downs through Gordon Creek, where the Yarralin is now, right up to Humbert River.

While we was down there at Humbert River waiting to get the cattle, Charlie Schultz, the manager there, sort of took pity on me—he knew that I was a good cattleman, he liked me—and he asked me, 'Could you stay on and work for me?'

I said, 'Yeah, okay.'

'But you must go with old Jack first,' he said. 'Take the cattle down to Wyndham, and after you've finished you can come back.'

I said, 'Okay.'

I didn't go droving very often because I was a real first-class qualified cattleman, and Vesteys said, 'He's too good a man to send him off droving. He's the man that gets a lot of cattle for us to make the properties pay.' But this time I went and we took twelve hundred head of bullock to Wyndham with old Jack Davidson. He was a very old man then, about seventy-odd, still droving cattle, and he was a bugger to drink metho. One time old Davidson had a wife, old Maggie—they were really married—and Maggie used to travel with him everywhere—from Delamere district and Victoria River Downs district right down to the other side of Mt Isa, right through the Barkly Tableland. She was a wonderful old lady. She was a drover. Old Jack used to always rely on her. He used to take twelve to fifteen hundred at a time and old Maggie was there with the stockwhip and a big hat on. She was a great girl for old Jack, and one time old Jack was on the soup, he was drunk with the metho, out at Delamere in 1959. Anyway, Jack was too full of metho and Maggie was on the metho too, and Wason Byers rides up to old Jack Davidson and he said, 'Jack, old Maggie dead, she got drowned in the waterhole.'

Old Jack gets up. He says, 'Get out of my camp. Go on, get out of my camp,' and old Byers can't explain to him that old Maggie got drowned in this little shallow water because she was full of metho. So Byers rang the cops up in Katherine, and the coppers went out to Delamere with the motor car with a box to put old Maggie in. When the police come out, old Jack was still stung. They brought old Jack in, and he didn't even know he was in the police car right up until he was in Katherine gaol. Then when he got sober and he woke up he was in gaol.

Old Jack Davidson was telling me, he said, 'First thing, when I was in gaol one mornin' I woke up, I was yellin' out to old Davey the old Aborigine to bring the horses in, and I looked up in the air and I can see the roof on top of me. I said to meself, "Where the hell I am? That's funny . . . I can't be in Delamere . . . this is a funny place."' He gets up and was walking around and around in the dark, and he waited till it breaking dawn and then he could see all the bars in the door. He said, 'Shit, I'm here in the gaol. I wonder where the hell is the gaol? Can't be at Timber Creek. I don't know where it'd be.'

When the police came around and brought the breakfast they said, 'Jack, you remember comin' in here?'

He said, 'No.'

They said, 'You remember old Mag died?'

Jack said, 'Oh he's in my camp.'

'He's in your camp all right, he's in a coffin.'

Old Jack said, 'What?'

'He's in the coffin because he drank and you drank. She got drowned in the shallow water. You lucky you still alive.' He was the metho king, and anyway he did three months in the prison, old Jack, for giving the grog to Maggie. It happened to be his wife, but if it would have been another outsider he would have got twelve months for it.

Jack used to like the opium, too, and this started one day when he was at Wave Hill, when he was camped there with all these other old-time drovers like old Owen Cummings and Jack Chuckabull, and another drover, old Charlie Swan, come along. Charlie Swan was the drover that got caught in the flood when old Sambo sang the rain at Wave Hill. He was a drover all his life, and he was always getting tangled up with the rum. He had a great big moustache and a big conkleberry pipe, you know, and a great big hat on top of that. He used to always walk around, head down, and he always drove a lot of cattle through Murranji right down Mt Isa way, and he was a wonderful old drover, old Charlie Swan. He used to smoke a helluva lot of smokes—he'd be puffing this pipe away nearly all day and night. He'd start off about four or five o'clock in the morning and won't stop till twelve o'clock in the night.

Anyway, Charlie comes up and says g'day to old Jack Davidson, and Charlie was smoking his pipe, and he had a funny smell coming out of that pipe, and Jack asked him what the tobacco was that he was smoking.

'Oh,' said Charlie, 'it's opium.'

See, Charlie Swan had been down to get some stores in Katherine, and as he was riding up the street he saw this Aboriginal woman smoking a big pipe. Charlie looked and she had a great big cigar thing, a long pipe, about 3 foot long, and she was puffing away, and old Charlie Swan said, 'Gawd strike me dead, I've seen some blokes that smoked pipes, but I haven't seen a pipe as long as that.' He walks over to this old Aboriginal woman who was sitting down there puffing away and he said, 'What you got in there, old lady?'

'Oh,' she said, 'I smoking a pipe.'

'A pipe!' he said. 'You call that a pipe? That's like a big log. Can I have a draw out of it?' The old Aboriginal woman gave him a taste and old Charlie Swan was puffing away there, and he said, 'Very nice smoke,' and he looked around and he seen these other old Aboriginal blokes there smoking through a bottle and he said, 'Gawd, what are you doing over here? What have you got in there? What you smoking? It's got a very strong smell.'

'Oh,' the Aboriginal bloke said, 'I smoking good smoke. Them old Chinese gave me.'

'Yeah?' old Charlie Swan reckoned, 'can I have a taste?' and old Charlie got into it puffing away there. 'Gawd!' old Charlie Swan reckons, 'that's the greatest one I ever smoked! It's very smelly, it's nice. What's the name of that?'

He said, 'Opium.'

'Opium?'

'Yeah. That off Chinese. It's a drug.'

'Oh, Gawd,' Charlie Swan said, 'where could I find the Chinese so I could get some opium off 'em?'

They said, 'Mostly all Chinese over at Pine Creek.'

See, a lot of Chinese come from overseas—they heard about a lot of minerals in Australia—and they were exploring a lot around the Pine Creek area for gold. They used Aborigines for labour because the Aborigine was the one that knew where all the minerals were in the country. They were very harmless, the old Chinese, though sometimes they used to work shit out of the old Aborigine, and they were a bit on the crabby side—very bad tempered. They get niggly over anything real quick and lose their block, and they just used to pick up a gun and shoot the old Aborigine. Then the blacks turned around and used to take all the Chinese into the hills and put a Chinese bloke in the lead, and then spear the old Chinese bloke. Or he'd be digging away with a pick and shovel or having lunch, or the old Chinese would lie down under a tree, and the next thing he'd have a spear stuck on his back or on his rib. They were very nasty towards the old Chinese.

Anyway, it was the Chinese who brought in the opium. Oh God! and the blacks right through in that area were mad about this opium. They used to love it. You could see the blacks throw the tobacco away and just race for this opium.

Anyway, old Charlie gets his stores and goes back to his camp at Wave Hill and Jack Davidson and the other drovers were asking about this opium. 'Now look,' said Charlie,' we're the white man and we been in this district for many years, and we know how to smoke pipe and cigarettes, and the black know about smoking cigarettes and pipe,' he said, 'but I come across one old Aboriginal woman there sitting down smoking this long 3-foot-long wood. She calls it a pipe but it looked like a big log to me,' he said, 'and I looked around and I seen this old other Aboriginal bloke smoking what they call opium through the bottle.'

Jack Davidson had a draw on Charlie's pipe, and it was making him all dreamy, and he said, 'God, I drink metho and essence of lemon and vanilla, but I must go down and look for some Chinese bloke. Wonder where they are?'

'Oh, they're down in Pine Creek area somewhere.'

So Jack Davidson was up and he rode over to Pine Creek, and he saw a line of Chinese there on the road digging away for a bit of gold. He rides up and says g'day and one of the old Chinese blokes said hello to him. He's sitting down having a yarn, and he was explaining to the Chinese that he was an old drover and they asked him where he was going and he said, 'Oh, I just come looking 'round down here.'

He pulled a cigarette out and an old Chinese bloke said to him, 'That stuff you smoking is no good.'

Jack Davidson sat down next to the Chinaman and he said, 'What sort of smoke do you smoke?'

I think this old Chinese was old Willy Lee Ting. He said, 'I'll give you something very good. If you find me gold I'll give you all this.'

Old Jack Davidson said, 'What is it?'

'You taste it,' he said.

Jack Davidson smoked it through the pipe. 'Oh,' he said, 'that's very nice.' His head was getting giddy and he was dreaming a lot of things and he reckoned it was great. Anyway, old Jack Davidson started exploring for gold. It looked funny, the old drover bloke exploring for gold, and Jack Davidson ended up getting a couple of boys looking for this gold. Anyway Jack Davidson goes back and he says to this old Chinese, 'I got about 10 ounces of gold in here.'

Old Willy was very pleased to see it and he give him this box full of opium. Jack Davidson was very pleased to get this opium off the Chinese and he come back to Katherine, picked up his stores there, packed them up in the pack bag, and away he went. He went along through Willeroo up to Montejinni right to Wave Hill, and when he got down there he was telling old Owen Cummins and old Charlie Swan and Jack Chuckabull, 'You know what happened when I get down to Pine Creek?' he said. 'The old Chinese bloke told me to look for gold,' he said, 'and I did, I found 10 ounces of gold and gave it to this old Chinese bloke and he was very proud to be getting this gold and he gave me this box of opium.'

They said, 'We must try it.'

He said, 'I had a go of it along the road here, and it was very nice,' and then they all had a go of it.

But old Jack Chuckabull reckons, 'God, I'd be better off drinking carbide and toothpaste to get drunk before I have a smoke of this opium.' But old Charlie Swan said it was always a very nice smoke, and he was smoking it all day. Strangers would say 'Jeez, what's that? You got opium in there, Charlie?'

'No, I got nothing, just the conkleberry pipe burning.'

'Oh,' they said, 'I think it smells a bit like opium.'

'No.'

He used to keep it always hid away, old Charlie, but he loved that old opium because he always used to come around and pick up the opium off the old Chinaman at Willeroo, old Eric Kim Sing. Anyway, when the opium ran out old Charlie had to stick to rum. He had a homemade brew from pumpkin, but he was really always on the opium. That's where old Charlie got cancer in the throat, and he died of that.

Anyway, I was droving with old Jack and he employed the Aborigine for a guide, to show him where the waterholes were, so they could have a drink for the cattle. See, the Aboriginal will always know where the waterholes are because the songline links with the waterhole. The songline is the song that in my Wardaman country was made by the black-headed python, when he made all the rivers and the waterholes, and he named them in his songlines. These songlines go all over the country, and when the songline comes to the boundary of Wardaman country, the next mob take it over, and this songline continues all the way to the coast. And the Aborigine who knows the songline can take the drover to all the waterholes along the way. They was a set route from when the Aboriginal was walking around for ceremonies and for trade, and that's the same route that they made the stock route out of when the cattle industry started to operate in this country—it was the old Aboriginal trade route.

So the drovers went along following the blackfella to the waterhole, and plonked his cattle there and drank all the water, and moved off to another waterhole. The bullocks used to walk across from Humbert River and over to Barrac Barrac, then they hit the road at Auvergne and goes to Wyndham that way, walking all day and resting at night.

At night-time you'd have a sleep for a couple of hours and then get up to watch the cattle and sing to keep them quiet. One old bloke always used to sing:

> *Brown doggy, quit now, shifting,*
> *Shuffling around, my horse is leg weary,*
> *I'm all done, time to lay down,*
> *Tomorrow we run,*
> *Lay down, lay down you little doggy,*
> *Lay down, lay down, oh bullock go to sleep now.*

That was a real old-time song. As a kid we sort of picked it up and we reckon that was a great song. It kept the cattle quiet. Then next morning at four o'clock they'll get the cattle moving, and they'll go along and they'll pull up for lunch, take their bullock into the waterhole and water the cattle till about two o'clock. Then they'll walk on to the overnight camp, and we'd be based there for the night watch again, and then next morning at four o'clock again they'll leave. That's the way the drover used to always operate.

There was a cook and six others for driving the cattle— one boss bloke and five others, sometimes half and half, black and white, sometimes less Aborigine, sometimes more Aborigine and a couple of whites, some was all Aborigine with just one white, you know. They carried about sixty horses—they had canteens to carry the water, and they had pack bags and pack sacks and pack saddles. If there was a road, like when after '51 a two-wheel track come along, they'd carry their food and stuff like this in a buggy with two draughthorses pulling the buggy. If you didn't have any powdered milk you always took one goat with you, or a chook to lay eggs, so you could have steak and eggs or something like that, or you could have fresh milk off the goat. For tucker the drover always had flour and tea and sugar, and a cook made a damper and stews in the camp oven—a good cook made custard as they're travelling.

I said to Jack Davidson, 'How much you get for taking bullock across from here?'

He said, 'Five bob a head for a hundred miles.'

Five bob wasn't big money of course—what's that? 50 cents a head these days for 160 kilometres—anyway, after they finished delivering the cattle over at Wyndham the drover would say, 'We'll store our horses into the paddock and let's go to the races. Let's have a break-up now,' and everyone used to go in to the racecourse. Of course the Aborigine in that time wouldn't drink, because we wasn't allowed to, so we'd just go down to have a look at the horses, just meet a friend and relations. But the European used to go in there and get on the piss and everyone was singing and fighting amongst themselves. Today, of course, when Aborigine take on the booze, they fighting amongst themselves too.

Anyway, we delivered to Wyndham—that was about 400 miles, not too far, it took six weeks to get there I reckon—and I come back down the river and I worked with old Charlie Schultz for a while, and oh! Charlie Schultz was a very hard man. 'Lundard' they called him. He was a *lundard*—a grumbly old thing. I got on all right with him but he was a very hard man on the Aborigine. He'd work the Aborigine from daylight till dark, no wages. I was only getting £9 a week then—about $18 a week—and the work was very hard too, with mean tucker—one slice of bread, a little slice of meat, and that's about all.

I was with Charlie on the cattle, and after the camp season was closed Charlie wanted some timber. There was me, Les Humbert and Larry Johns, and old Darby the old police tracker now today at Timber Creek—we went across to Murranji and cut over two thousand lancewood rails to put up the stockyards at Bullita and Humbert River. We had an old blitz truck—it's still over there laying down there at Bullita—and we was carting rail with that. But I said, 'Oh, this is no good, I might shift over to another place,' and I ran into another bloke called Ivor Hall.

He said, 'Can you come down and do all the saddles for me?'

I said, 'Okay,' and I took a job on at Killarney with Ivor Hall. He had no homestead, just a bough shelter, and I was doing up a lot of saddles there right through till March 1960, and then Vesteys offered me a job again to Limbunya, and I went over there to Limbunya on a Conair airplane, back to Vesteys again. I was supervisor again and then I was with a different tribe of Aborigine—they call themself Gurindji—and after that I come back to Katherine and I took a job on with Mataranka, in 1961, doing the saddles there.

Chapter Nineteen

YOU BATTLED WITHOUT ME

I hadn't seen my old man, old Bill Harney, for a long time, and then one day I saw him there at Mataranka, in 1961, and that was the last time I ever saw old Bill Harney.

I had heard about what my father was doing from an old Aboriginal man I met called Kudekudeka, from down the desert way. Big upstanding bloke he was. He's an old desert blackfella, but he's dead now I think. Anyway, he said to me, 'Oh, Billarni, he's my boss down Ayers Rock way.' See, my old man had taken a job. He was first ranger at Ayers Rock, and Kudekudeka said to me, 'Well Billarni been askin' me to go out to Ayers Rock. "I want to write up a book," that's what old Bill Harney said to me. I said to Bill, "I'll take you out to place and show you a good spring there, you can sit down there."'

Somewhere, sometimes, a small idea arises, that gives birth to unforseen events.

I was out visiting my friends the Webbs at Jay Creek, which is a government settlement thirty miles (forty-eight kilometres) westward from Alice Springs . . . a utility van pulled up outside the main gate and in walked Harry Giese, the Director of Welfare in the Northern Territory of Australia . . . the conversation got around to the Native Reserves which were at that time in the public eye. The main part of the talk was the newly transferred portion of the south-western Aboriginal reserve to the Ayers Rock—Mount Olga National Park, an area of 400 square miles (1032 square kilometres) was to be preserved as a place where tourists could go to see the scenic wonders which were slowly drawing travellers from the cities to these hitherto unknown areas.

During the conversation I was asked, Would I care to go out to be the first ranger of the area? Being out of work at the time I naturally jumped at the opportunity of going to a place I had never visited, but had heard so much about both from the white travellers and from the Loritdja Aborigines who once lived in that locality . . .

As there was no dwelling for the new ranger at Ayers Rock I was issued with a ten-by-twelve tent and fly which would be my living quarters and office . . . and a list of instructions as to what I had to do as regards control of the area. I must issue permits to people entering the National Park; native cave art must be protected and nothing removed from the area . . . I had already written away to my friends in the right places about the geology, history, and botany of the Centre and Ayers Rock, but still the ritual story of the Aborigines remained a mystery to me.

From W.E. Harney, *To Ayers Rock and Beyond*,
Lansdowne Publishing, Sydney, 1995

Anyway, one day they jumped on the old camel and they rode straight across country all the way down to Ayers Rock, and old Bill said, 'Oh this is ideal place for me to sit down to write a book.' Along with Kudekudeka there were other Aborigines all walking around down there, sitting down there, all working for old Bill, building up this donga, and he was sitting down writing a story about that country.

After he finished that book he took a few pictures of Ayers Rock and he come back to Alice Springs and said, 'Look, I been out in the country, I got my little camp built up over there in a beautiful spring, and that hill over there it's a very interesting hill for people to come down to have a look. A very interesting hill! Should come a national park.' And they couldn't believe him. He said, 'I'll show you the picture,' and he showed them the pictures of this Ayers Rock. That was around 1956, I think.

This Northern Territory government in Darwin flew over and had a look. They said, 'This is a ideal hill all right.' Old Bill had his little tin shed there, and he was writing books about what he was doing in there. They said, 'We'll push a road through and then a bus can get in, and people can climb up to have a look at the hill,' and this is what they did. Then they said to old Bill, 'We'll put you here as a ranger,' and he come the first ranger at Ayers Rock and this old boy Kudekudeka stuck to him, all the way.

And that's how I knew where my old man was, and when I was at Mataranka in '61, I was in the pub there one day and a couple of young fellas pulled up there, and we were talking and they said, 'We're anthropologists way down there at Ayers Rock.'

I said, 'Oh, you down at Ayers Rock?' (I didn't tell them that Bill was my dad.) I said, 'Old Bill Harney over there, he's an anthropologist.'

The first thing they said was, 'Oh, that old bastard, he's not a anthropologist, we are the anthropologist!'

I said, 'Oh yes? How'd you know about being an anthropologist? What rule do you know?' I said, 'Bill was with Aboriginal all his life. He has to be an anthropologist because he was taught and learnt from the Aboriginal, learnt the spiritual side and everything with the Aborigine.'

'Oh,' he said, 'that old bullshitting bastard, he talks your head off. He's a know-all fuckin' thing.'

I said, 'Oh yeah?'

They said, 'He's not gunna last down there, he's getting old and he's gunna get out soon.'

I don't know who they were, but I went crook at them. 'How do you know everything about being an anthropologist!' Of course one of these young fellas might have been trying to push Bill out. They might have been accusing old Bill to upset him a bit. Anyhow, that's the time old Bill was getting sad, and then he went away to die.

Old Bill Harney describes his time as ranger at the rock as a time of contending with rude tourists and religious zealots who wished to decry the Aboriginal story of Uluru. After leaving, he prefaced his book *To Ayers Rock and Beyond* with the words:

> *'For each man kills the thing they love,*
> *By all let this be heard.' (Wilde)*

Jan Wositzky

I was still in Mataranka when I saw him last, and someone in the pub there said, 'Your dad just gone through, he's coming back in a couple of days. I told him you were here. He said, could you come round and see him.'

I said, 'All right.'

The bus used to camp overnight at Mataranka and a couple of days later, one afternoon, he was there and he was very pleased to see me. Him and Doug Lockwood were together—he used to write a few books about the Northern Territory too, old Doug Lockwood—and they invited me to go in and have a meal in the lounge, and I sat down and I had a feed with them. He just said, 'I'm pleased with you, you come good, and you operate by yourself.'

Doug Lockwood was his mate, a good bloke, very nice bloke, you know, and he was very surprised that I was Bill's son, and Bill was very proud of me there talking to him. Anyway, old Doug Lockwood said, 'By jeez, he does look a bit like you all right. How come you didn't put him in the book?'

Old Bill said, 'Was one of those things. I was in the Welfare and didn't want to bring it out because you know the rule they had, because the Welfare was not to be associated with any Aboriginal lady.'

Well I listened to them talking about one book old Bill was writing and he said, 'I'm going down to Queensland to live down there, at Mooloolaba, and if you want to come down there you can drop around.'

I said, 'Okay,' but I was stuffing around with Vesteys, and it was a helluva long way to go down there to the coast, and the next I heard he'd finished, see.

W.E. Harney died on New Year's Eve, 1962. He was found dead in bed the next day, beside him a notebook, in which the last entry read, 'As I sat at my neighbour's table I felt queer. The next thing I knew, Doctor Winn Fowles was leaning over me and gave me an injection. As in a dream I heard him say, "He has had a heart attack. He must have rest." '

From W.E. Harney and D. Lockwood, *The Shady Tree*
Lansdowne Publishing, Sydney, 1995

I got a tombstone photograph. One bloke sent it down. He's buried somewhere about 60 mile from Brisbane. His sister was

there but I don't know that old girl. In my opinion he was
fantastic, straight up top. He never bashed me up. That time
at Mataranka I said, 'I better give you the money that I owe
you from that block of land in the Fitzmaurice.'

He said, 'No, don't ever give me any money, because I
never ever did give you any money. That's yours. I never really
gave you anything when you was a kid, because you was
nowhere near me. You battled it out without me. Don't give
me any money, that yours.'

I said, 'Oh all right,' and that was the last that I saw him,
in 1961.

Chapter Twenty

YOU GUNNA GET MARRIED

I did the saddles at Mataranka right up till June 1961, and then I went cypress pine cutting with Russ Jones in the Moil Tableland there, and I was a great axeman in my time. I used to drop twenty big trees down and drag them off in the scrub to the ramp and stack them up—full trees, 40 to 50 foot long.

When cutting the cypress pine an old bloke called Steve told me, 'When you cutting the pine don't drink water because you get cramp in your hand, and you get very shaky. You must drink cold tea, don't put any sugar in it, that's to keep your system very good.'

He was cutting a lot of timber in Victoria, up in the hill country with the axe, and he used to climb halfway up in the tree and cut the tree down. Well he taught me to do that and soon as we'd knock off he'd say to me, 'You gotta have one nip of this metho, take all the ache and pains off the bones, you know,' and every night we did that, after the cutting, have a cup of metho, not a full one, but good enough to relieve your aching bones. We used to drink metho with coffee—'coffee royal' we used to call it. And sometimes we used to make toast, eat the toast, then drink the metho as well. We'd call that 'metho on toast'. About 10 minutes after, you start to get hungry and you go down and cook your steak, big mob you cook, and you eat well, and you lay down and you can hardly get up—it gets you real drunk, proper drunk. Then you wake up next morning fit, ready for more axe work. It relieves your bones, it goes right through your system and cleans you right out. You're working real hard and you are real tired, and sometimes you get restless so you can hardly sleep—you overwork yourself—but you hit yourself with that metho and oh jeez! you can feel it go through you. Number one. It cures you.

Anyway, come Christmas on the cypress pine and we couldn't get a cargo of grog for Christmas because the river was up, and we said, 'We gotta have something special for drinking for Christmas.'

There was this 44-gallon drum of metho there. It was for the lantern and to iron the clothes—we just used to put metho in the iron and light it up and iron our clothes. Anyway, someone said, 'Oh what's that?'

'Forty-four of metho.'

'Oh well, that'll do,' and we drank the 44 drum, took us a week to drink it, about ten of us drunker than the dogs, Jesus Christ yeah! We drank a 44-gallon drum, I tell you. See, you can get blind as a bat with metho today, and tomorrow morning you wake up with eyes so clear you can see everything. Not crook. Fit! But with beer and rum you wake up and oh, you got headache and everything. And if you was on the grog for a week or so and you feel you can't eat, you feel terrible, well you get about 3 inches of metho into a big cup, put a dash of water on it, fill him right up, hold your breath, down the whole lot non-stop like drinking water, put the cup down, let your breath out, and you get that big shiver. Well jeez! They reckon you go blind with the metho, but I'm not blind and I drank the 44 drum! Jeez, we drank it in gallons.

Anyway, after Christmas it was back on the axe work and I loved it you know, because I was in good prime then. I used the axe non-stop. I was a very fit man. I got £15 a week—that's $30 a week—and that was big money in that time.

Then in 1962, my mum come along and told me, 'You gunna get married.'

And old Joe Jomornji said, 'You gunna get married.'

I said, 'What I want to get married for?'

They said, 'You gotta get married because we fixed it up with that mob you gunna get married to.' They wanted me to marry Ida—we'd grown up together, she was from Manbulloo—

and old Joe sat down with Ida's relations and had a yarn and they all agreed. Neither Ida or me knew what was going on.

Before Ida, I was promised to another old lady called *Yiwarninji*, because it was always the law that the young boy about eighteen marries the old lady about sixty year old, and the middle-aged man he marries a young one too. This was going to happen after my initiation, with another ceremony when the old people sing the *bundimi* song, and all the old ladies dance strip-bollocky naked with their tits hanging down and clapping their legs, and they bring a mussel and rub it all over your face and they say, 'Now you call out *'mamburru'*.' *Mamburru* means fanny. They say, 'You call out *mamburru* loud so everyone can hear you,' and you call it out about twenty times, and they are singing the song, and then they say, 'You've had a good look at them, therefore you're cleared to get married,' after that you're allowed to go and sleep with the woman—she might be sixty, seventy-year-old lady.

But first you got to have the tribal mark—that's the cuts around the chest and the belly and the shoulders—and then they know you've been through the *bundimi* and you can go into the women's camp then. Before that you are not allowed to look at them, you're unregistered. Anyway, after that the old lady is your wife then, and she teaches you everything, and you must stay with her right up till she dies. Then you can pick up another girl, a young one.

Anyway, my promised old lady died just before I went through that ceremony, and straight after I moved from the Aboriginal camp to the white man's camp, and that's how come I was never married with the old lady. Then my dad come along and told me that I was going to marry Ida. Her Aboriginal name was *Wugogunn*, and she was promised to another man, but he died too, and they told Ida that we were going to get married, and I said, 'Oh, all right.'

Then they had this big ceremony. It's not a dangerous ceremony, they just have a normal open ceremony—there's a corroboree going on, lots of bush tucker, everybody happy, and they say, 'Here, both of you gotta sit down.' Next they start off singing and everybody is happy, dancing and blowing didgeridoos, and after that was finished they said, 'All right, youse can go.'

Anyway we was quite happy, married in the Aboriginal way, and we continued for a long while, and then the Welfare started chasing me around the country. See, part-Aborigines weren't allowed to marry an Aboriginal lady, and I was classed as a part-European, and the Welfare went over and seen our parents and they wanted to take us away from each other. They reckoned if the Aborigine classed as a part-European was to marry an Aborigine, we might have a dark child, and they didn't want to see more dark Aborigine kid in the country. They only wanted to see full Aborigine marry the full-blooded Aborigine, and that's why they came looking into me and my missus Ida.

And my mum and old Joe said, 'No you can't take 'em off because they get married Aboriginal way, and they gotta stay that way.'

The Welfare said, 'Well, if you gunna get proper married why can't they get married proper European way? That way they can't get touched.'

Old Joe and my mum said, 'Oh well all right, we'll organise something.' We wasn't in any religion or anything, so we just put ourselves in the Catholic Church in Katherine. The whole family come when we got married, and we fit in the corner and then we got married by Father Worman. We didn't know what was going on. The Welfare bloke Creed Lovegrove was there when we got married, just to make sure we signed the paper, and after that they let us go.

After we got married I joined with Les Turley shooting crocodiles down the Fitzmaurice. I was rowing the dinghy, and we would be shooting man-eating crocodiles, big salty crocodiles.

We always had one man standing up in the front with the spotlight on his forehead, and two harpoon men, one on each side. We'll row along and if this bloke with the light saw a crocodile there on your left or right, I'd turn the boat left slowly and he'd say, 'Yeah that's it, go straight ahead.' The big one is the dangerous one you had to shoot through the eye so the bullet can go right through his brains—if you shoot him in the forehead the bullet will just ricochet because his head was rock hard. They get in under the boat sometimes and they tip the boat, but we used to hang on—whether he tipped it over or not I'll be still hanging on. We went right through from October till December, and I was on good money—£50 a week in the finger.

Chapter Twenty-one

ALL GONE

Then I went back to poddy-dodging with Tex Moar till March '63, and that's when I went across to Flora Valley with Vesteys again, right through till 1965. I was a supervisor there again, the boss's man in the camp in Flora Valley. We were branding cattle and mustering and moonlighting and night-watching cattle, delivering the cattle to the drover. Then all of a sudden, delivering the bullock to the drovers stopped, and the cattle train come in. That was in 1964. We started loading the bullocks onto the road train, and old Buntine was the fella with the first road train out my way.

He started off with nothing and gradually old Buntine worked himself right into it and got a big lot of transports—cattle trucks and everything, and before he died, just the other day, he was a multimillionaire. He cut all the drovers out and took all the cattle in the cattle trucks. One time cattle used to walk from the Territory up to Queensland right down to Rockhampton and Townsville and across to the meatworks, and walk all the way down to Wyndham meatworks—there were never any other meatworks around here. Then when Buntine cuts all the drovers right out with the cattle trucks, he had it all sewn up. After that, no more drovers. Now the the stock route from the Kimberley down to Halls Creek district and right down to Wyndham, and the Canning stock route, well, that's closed. The Murranji stock route up to the Barkley Tablelands, through Sudan to right down to Dajarra, that's lonesome today, because the road train took over. The drovers' Condamine bells, they're staying still—no more noise for the Condamine bell. Now we miss that because we always used to hear that bell and you'd know that the drover had turned up. Now all you could hear was the roaring of the bitumen.

Then in 1966 came the Gurindji walk-off from Wave Hill. I was at Flora Valley—I was still with Vesteys in 1966—and what happened, we went down early to Negri Races, and the Wave Hill mob come down there. In that time they was getting two pound a week, eight pound a month, and they was a bit concerned about it, because they had to buy tobacco and stuff like this with the two pound a week. Anyway they was telling us then at Negri Races that they were unhappy, and when they go back to Wave Hill they all went on strike.

Vincent Lingiari was boss leader for Gurindji and at that time he was in Darwin in the hospital, and he ran into Dexter Daniels, a bloke who used to work for the union mob, and Frank Hardy, and somebody else—I don't know this other man. Anyway, they flew across to Wave Hill and when they landed over there then they told Vincent what to do.

Anyway, this one morning all the stockmen just bailed up, they didn't go to work, and the cook's ringing bells and no girls come down to waitress, to lay the plates and stuff out. Anyway, Tom Fisher the manager was waiting in the house and there was nobody moving, and anyway he drove down to the Aboriginal camp and he said to everybody, 'What's going on? This not a holiday, youse gotta come to work. Now come on,' he said, 'it's work time.'

Old Vincent Lingiari said, 'We want £25 a week. If not, we don't go to work.'

'Oh!' and old Tom said, 'we can't give you £25 a week, that's too much money for you, too many of youse here.'

Old Vincent said, 'Oh well, we going down to the river because we not going to work for £2 a week,' and they all headed down to the river where the original old Wave Hill police station was, and they were all sitting down on the river there.

Anyway, the travelling boss, Peter Morris, called in—the travelling boss will go all over the property and if the manager made a mistake, well he'll fire him. Anyway, they rang the travelling boss up and told him that all the blacks had flared up, and he come down the river and talked to Vincent. He said, 'We give you a feed, what about coming back to work?'

Old Vincent said, 'No, we not go to work, unless we get £25 a week.'

Dexter Daniels was there and he said, 'These boys are not going to work at all. From the start they work for nothing. They made money for Vesteys, they made heaps of money for Vesteys and they're not getting any money at all. These boys not will work in the property any more.'

Old Tom Fisher went back to the station and he said, 'Well, I'm not gunna manage any more because the blacks is all gone,' and they put this other old bloke in there, old Frank Wilmington, and they said to Frank, 'You manage the station.' They knew he always got on well with the Aborigine, and they said to Frank, 'Try if you could bring them back to work.'

Well old Frank goes down to the river to see if he can con them into coming back to work. They said to Frank, 'We like you old man, but the company not paying us good money, we not going back to work. We have to be on £25 a week.' That was big money, I wasn't getting that much either, by myself, but that's what they walked off for.

When this happened I was over at Flora River, and when we heard about it we felt a bit sad—we hoped the other Aborigines would not do the same thing. We felt, because the Aborigines belonged to the area, in the first place they should have asked the property owner to give them a small block of land to live on. And if the Aborigines had to be on £25 a week— and that's for three hundred Aborigines all working for £25 a week—that's a lot of money.

Then old Tom Fisher, he'd been in this country with this mob a long time, after they walked off he felt very sad about it and it broke his heart. Old *Baburdirda* they called him in Wardaman because he had hair only around the side of his head. He went back down south to New South Wales and he died. Sort of broke his feelings, because he got on well with the Aborigines, and the Aborigines really liked him as well.

Anyway, this Vincent Lingiari said, 'We want land. We shall have an area of Gurindji, and area for Wardaman, for Ngarinman, for Ngaliwurru, Djaru, and for all them other different languages all around in here.' See, all of the Aboriginal land was covered by the pastoralists' property. Different to Arnhem Land because it's no use for cattle, it's rubbish country. It's only good for lizards and wallaby, and no good for cattle. You won't fatten the cattle up because it's speargrass, and that's why they left that area to become Aboriginal land.

But where Vincent Lingiari walked off, that was covered by the pastoral property, and that's when Mr Whitlam came along, and of course he was right behind them then. He was talking about the legal rights, about the award wages, and that's when they broke the Aboriginal working system, and the Aboriginal was taken away from the land in many properties— when the award wages come in. That was in 1968, and the pastoral properties said, 'We can't employ you all because there's too many of you. You gunna cost too much money.'

Some properties carried over five hundred Aborigines, some three hundred to two-fifty, seventy to one hundred Aborigine on many properties, and it was too much for one station to employ that many. Before they would employ the whole lot, all two hundred of them—in the house, doing the fencing, some employed in the stock camp, about eighteen to twenty about around the house, cleaning up, cutting firewood and all this sorta thing. They was only getting a feed and a supply of clothing and they were happy too, as happy Aborigine as ever seen. But in 1968 when that award come in, well the property owner said, 'God! Too many for me to pay this award wages, about $36 a week for three hundred of 'em! That's too much! He'll have to go to town and the government can look after 'im.'

Well, all the Aborigines didn't want to leave the country, but the pastoral properties were saying, 'Oh, we can't have you runnin' around in the bush scarin' cattle, makin' a mess in the country and all this sorta thing.' They wasn't going to make a mess, but this European idea was that Aboriginals make a mess of the country, and the pastoral bloke said, 'Youse go to town,' and then all the Aborigines they come in to live in the town.

Then the booze come in, in 1964, and everyone was living on in town area, and the good class of Aboriginal stockman was finished up—he become a booze-artist in town.

Before that no Aborigine was allowed to drink, and if any white man got caught supplying the grog to the Aborigine then the white man got sent to gaol for six months. But we used to get it all right. And when the stockmen came to town to do a bit of freeing up, they'd get on the booze and go to someone's backyard and have a bullfight. This was a happy-go-lucky drinking time. Everyone used to go out and have a very big fire, and lots of rib bones were thrown in the coals, and everyone was sitting around with a carton of beer—drink up—then everyone takes their shirt off, and says, 'Oh well, we're going to do the bullfight.' Then you get down on your hands and knees and make out you're a bull, and two people start charging in, head to head, knocking the person over, and the one on top is the winner. If anyone had a long nose he had a lot of scatches on his nose, and if another bloke had a short nose he had a lot of scratches on his forehead. You'd have sore ribs, sore knees, from the bullfighting in this little ring, human to human.

Myself, I started drinking in 1961. We bought a big case of beer—twenty-four large bottles, and I had a couple of bottles out of it and I thought that was it. In our time we didn't go out to drink to get blotto and go berserk, we only drank enough to keep us going and be happy, and didn't take any grog back to the home, and we always saddled up for work the next day.

I stopped later because after I drank all these spirits—rum, whisky, brandy, metho—I saw a lot of good men just dragged away by the grog. One old fella told me, 'Young fella, you mustn't drink too much. I saw the good man destroyed by the grog. This grog is like throwing a line in the water to catch a fish. The grog got its line to drag you into the hotel. Once you taste one you want more to get blotto. 'Course you don't know what you're doing, you could have an argument and you'll end up stabbing someone with a knife.'

Then some Aboriginal bloke used to always trade his lady to another man for grog, so when I was drinking during the 'sixties I said to myself, 'Well I must think back now to what the old bloke told me. What I can see in front of me, I don't want to get in that mischief. I must give the grog away.' When we come in from the bush to drink, we got drunk over one or two nights, then we were back in the bush for two years. We didn't worry about grog going back, and after two years we go back and get on the grog again for another couple of nights. 'Well,' I thought, 'I must give the grog away for good. I must go back to the bush with my own spiritual way and stay off the grog for ever and ever, to keep the wisdom to keep me going so I can see the changes,' and I give the grog away and now I can live longer. And when I gave the grog away I started all me own businesses, and I kept the cultural side alive, and I push my kids real hard to keep away from the booze. Me and my missus, we don't drink at all. Thousands around us and we're the only two sitting in the middle not taking any notice, just trying to pull everyone into gear.

Anyway, when this new law come in and the pastoral industry said, 'You can go into town and the government might be able to help you to a feed, but we can't have you here,' and the government said, 'Well youse gunna be equal now because you got equal rights to drink beer, and you got award wages, same as the white man—you gunna carry on in the white way now'—well, that's the way the Aborigines lost double. They were in the town off their land, and lost their full Aboriginal culture when the booze come in—that's when it broke their marriage and initiation and all that sort of thing. And when they got their legal right for drinking in 1964, the Aboriginal was fighting, and they finished up in gaol for killing themselves, and today there is more Aboriginal people in prison than what there was in the early days.

Then the helicopter come in, taking over from the stockmen, and the stockmen were closed down. In the bush the
bronco yard just collapsed, and the white ants went through
where we used to brand cattle. They don't brand the cows the
traditional way any more, like how we used to let the cow out
of the yard and graft the mother and calf together and leave
them mothered up—you don't see them any more. Today the
helicopters just run the cattle into the yard and they brand the
cows and they open the gate and away the cows go.

And they're not very good stockmen today. They think
they're a stockman, but they're not—they're not a stockman
like we were. The traditional stockman was a very good stockman—we shod our horses and went out looking for the cattle
in the long grass and in the scrub, and picked them up and
brought them back into the yard, and they were good cattle.
But now today, the people in the property rely on the helicopter, and by the time the cattle are into the yard their loins
are buggered and they just die straight away because he's over-
heated, with the tongue flapping. They wouldn't do that in the
early days. We weren't allowed to push the cattle like you're
playing football, otherwise we got in trouble over it. But today,
they do what they like, they couldn't give a damn how many
cows die in the yard.

Today, no stock camp. Nothing in the country for
branding in the open yard—that's gone. Night watching,
that's gone. Shoeing up the horses—the Aborigine they knew
their job shoeing up the horses—that's gone. They're not
shoeing horses on the property these days. All they do is
just get a saddle and ride anything. No more windmill
pumping the water now—they got all these solar things.
When the cattle industry was operating, lots and lots of
people had jobs. There was lots of stockmen around the
countryside, all over. Now there's no more jobs for anybody
in the country—white or black. A lot of property owners
have gone broke—their properties are for sale all over the
countryside. In some places they're starting up tourism and
there's just a little bit of the cattle industry now. I think

there's only 3 per cent the Aborigine goes to stock camp today, and 97 per cent of Aborigines are in town. Long time ago, 100 per cent Aborigine was all operating in the stock camp. Now the property just employ five or six, that's all.

Chapter Twenty-two

MOTHER AND FATHER, SAME TIME

I was still with Vesteys in 1966, and then old Reg Durack came along. He's the brother to old Mary Durack—Mary writes a book, too—and Reg picked me up, and I was with old Duracks from 1966 until 1974.

I got into a bit of trouble once there too, when I was supervising Durack's stock camp at Amanbidji. At the end of '67 I came in for a bit of a holiday to Katherine and I took a job on at Katherine store, and Cyril Millwood, he was the butcher, he knew me pretty well, and he asked me to go out and knock off a killer. We used to knock off a killer now and again, and anyway, this time I knocked this killer off and some bloke squealed on me. I had already gone back to Amanbidji for old Durack, and I was working on the bore when one of the CIB arrived.

I said, 'Hello.'

He said, 'Hello.'

I said, 'Where are youse going?'

He said, 'We came down to see you.'

I said, 'Oh, okay.' I knew what it was about straight away, and they took me back to Timber Creek and they give me a feed. They didn't lock me up that night—just put me in the cell but left the door open. The next day the police brought me up halfway to Katherine. The policeman had a revolver in his hand and when we stopped to rest he was firing at a rock close by, to show how accurate he was with the gun.

I said to the policeman, 'Don't shoot that rock, the bullet might ricochet and hit one of us.'

The policeman said, 'Oh, I never thought of that,' and we continued on up to the King River. The police said to me,

'If you tell me the truth and show me where the carcass is, I might be on your way, it might be good for you.'

I said, 'Okay,' and took them around and showed them where the head of the cow was under this tree.

He said, 'How did you shoot this under the tree here? Look like someone drove this cow to you.'

I said, 'No. What I did, I left my car in the river crossing and I went down and rubbed myself all over with mud, because it'll take the human smell off. Then I went up a tree and waited for the cow to come. I was sitting there for an hour, and old cow was gradually walking right up towards me. When he got closer I shot him. Then I came down and skinned him, and took all the meat into the town and gave it to Cyril Millwood. That's when I went out bush and you came along and got me.'

He said, 'Okay.'

Anyway, the first hearing was in Katherine, and I came out on a $100 bail. Then I had to come into the big Supreme Court of Darwin, and they had the evidence of the cow bones, and they put me up in the box. They said, 'How do you plead?'

I said, 'Guilty.'

And the judge read out, 'This man, Bill Harney, he worked for Vesteys for twenty years, now he's working at Kildurk Station with Mr Durack, one of the old pioneers. Also, when Mr Harney came into the town he worked at the police station at Katherine. He works very hard. The sweat was pouring out of him, no muck around for working was Mr Harney. No need for Bill Harney to go to gaol for driving around with this crew. Therefore, we let you out on good behaviour, on the bond, for eighteen months.' And they let me out!

Well I continued on working for Durack, and that was when my first two boys were born. First Billy in April 1971—Ida came to Darwin and he was born there—and later, in July 1972, Ida had another little boy, Roderick, in Katherine.

I stayed with Durack till 1974, and I went over to Kunun-urra, and that's when I was working for the Ord River farmer. I had never been on a tractor before, for ploughing the soil or harvesting and combining and all that, but I just jumped on a tractor and away I went operating a Massey Ferguson—ploughing, harvesting and growing the crops, combining, planting seeds, harvesting peanuts, mung beans, sorghum, oats, wheat and all sorts of things, sunflower, I was doing the lot.

I learned all that myself, then when I left the Ord River farmer I did a little bit of a job with Ord River Engineering—cutting and welding—and I became a small welder. From there I went across to Karl Dickie—a bloke that owns Kununurra Air Charter now today—and he had a farm at Packsaddle Plains, and he had a mob of stud cattle to be looked after. I was over there from 1976 to '77, then a bull kicked my hand while I was feeding him and he broke my right arm, and I ended up coming into the hospital. Of course the bone never got healed up, and around about the end of '78 I came in to Katherine. My missus Ida had some relations at Barunga and we went across over there.

Barunga is an Aboriginal settlement. Old Bill Harney set it up in the old Welfare days. It used to be called Bamyili, and that word doesn't mean anything, so they changed it to Barunga. Barunga means a meeting place for trade—in the European way it's like 'annual general meeting'. Anyway, over there at Barunga I was just sitting down in the camp and I took a job on in the garage, and I come to be like a mechanic. One old bloke taught me how to pull a motor down, and put it back together—and then at Barunga I was sort of operating the garage by myself, and as I went along I was learning to be a mechanic, and that's where I was teaching other Aborigine blokes to become a mechanic. They reckon I was a great mechanic, but I just learned by myself.

Then in early 1979, one night we went to sleep early, and I woke up at three o'clock in the morning, and Ida, my wife, she was dead and gone. I couldn't believe it. She just died. I had to race over in the middle of the night and ring the cops. Then the police came down. They rang an ambulance and the ambulance comes down, and it picked her up and took her away. Of course I was questioned next day. She always had a lot of headaches, and we couldn't work out what the headaches were for. She'd been taking Aspro over Aspro, and we'd taken her to the hospital a few times to check on the headache, and the doctor couldn't find anything. 'Oh well,' we said, 'might be just a headache.'

We had to wait a couple of weeks for the post-mortem, and I still couldn't work it out what killed her, and then they told us it was a tumour on the brain. They told me the tumour works from the brain right down, and eats the spine in the back of the neck, then he drips like gangrene in there, and then it just puts them off.

Well, I felt a bit sad for a start off, but I was lucky I had the two boys, Billy and Roderick, and they kept me sort of happy and under control. It was right. Then the Welfare come along to take the kids off me, and I said, 'No, I won't give my boys to the Welfare. I'll just keep 'em by myself. I want to teach them something.'

The Welfare said, 'How could you teach 'em by yourself? You'd be out working and the kids'd be lost.'

'Well,' I said, 'I can become a mother and a father, same time.'

Well I used to get up first thing in the morning, about four o'clock, and cook up their breakfast. Then when it was time for me to go to work I used to get them up, and they used to go to school and I'd go to work. Then of course I come home a bit later, but they used to be there before me and they'd be waiting around, and when I come home I'll cook up their tea and wash their clothes for school again. That's the way I was mother and father by myself. Big job, very hard, you know, but it's not impossible. Other people say, 'We give the kid away to someone else to look after them,' but not me. I looked after them by myself, and they're still here with me today.

Both went to the Open College to learn about being a boilermaker and carpenters and all that, and then I said, 'Oh well, I got to swing you into another job now, to become a stockman.' So I boot them out to King River to do a stockman's course. They were doing the stockman's jobs like what

I did, but I was learning the bush way and they was taught in the European way. Another part-Aborigine bloke, old Bill Fordham—he's the son from old Fordham the poddy-dodger—he was teaching them about shoeing up horses and breaking in horses and mustering cattle all through the Wet, and all this sort of thing. Now my sons they are qualified stockmen and they won the Queen's Medal. They come up first class, and I'm pleased with them for what they come up as. I thought they were just going to collapse altogether when their mother died, but they didn't.

Chapter Twenty-three

MY PROPER COUNTRY NOW

After my first missus Ida died, I came into Katherine at the end of 1979, and that's the time that I come across the other missus of mine, my wife today, Dixie. I needed a mother to look after those two boys, and Dixie was a promised marriage of mine. We got married the traditional Aboriginal way from her father, and also in the Catholic Church. We had a right-hand man and a best lady, who were Arthur Palmer and Toni Bauman—that was Toni who gave me the cassettes to get this book started.

Anyway, Dixie and I, we went to Kildurk and we worked there from 1980 till '81. Then Arthur and Toni they brought us into Katherine in September 1981, and I said to Dixie, 'Well, everyone else is claiming the land. You follow me, I want a land claim on my country, back of the Flora.'

She said, 'All right.'

The Federal Government's Northern Territory Land Rights Act of 1976 enabled Aborigines who could prove an unbroken spiritual affiliation to their country to claim back unalienated crown land.

Jan Wositzky

We heard about the land rights when they first formed the Northern Land Council, and people was talking about claiming land in different areas and straight afterwards the anthropologists Athol Chase and Betty Mehan came down and seen me about the Upper Daly Land Claim, and they got around asking everybody, 'Who this land belong to?'

Everybody said, 'Belong to Bill Harney Dreaming.'

They said, 'Oh yeah.'

And old Tarpot, my grandfa, says, 'That's his father's

country—that's where his big totem is, all the Dreaming sites. He take it up from his father, old Joe Jomornji.'

Then Athol and Betty came up to me and they asked me, 'You got anything to do with back of Flora?'

I said, 'Yeah, that's my proper Dreaming there.'

'You know all the history?'

I said, 'Yeah, I know all the history.'

'Oh well, it's up for the land claim. You want to land claim it?'

'All right,' I said, 'we've got all these children coming up, we must take them back to the bush to show them the history and their heritage in the country, their story, their songline, and do lots of ceremonies.' That's what we wanted the land for. We said, 'When they grow up in town they won't know nothing. We want the land.'

They said, 'If you don't get this the Northern Territory government will still take it and sell it to somebody else.'

See, first the NT government was saying that Aboriginal hasn't got a sacred site at all in this country, because no sacred site was mentioned in the early days. But Aboriginals were living in the property and doing the sacred law at the sacred site in the bush and they wouldn't tell the white man that we got sacred law business over there. The pastoral managers knew a bit about this sacred law, but they didn't know anything about a sacred bush site. Then when everyone moved into the town in 1968 and they couldn't go back out again, the NT government was saying, 'Oh, no sacred site in the bush, nothing in there.'

Now a sacred site is more or less a rocky site in the hill country and there's no rubbish goes through it. The sacred site was kept really under control when the Aborigine was around the country, but when the people left there around 1968 to come into town, the kangaroos just took over, sleeping under the ledge of the rocks, and cattle went in and started licking all these paintings. Then straight after 1968 the bulldozer went through a lot of sacred country, and many sacred sites were destroyed. But my sites are okay because they're not close to the bitumen. Anyway, Athol and Betty said, 'Best to fight the government and get your land, otherwise they'll destroy all your Dreamtime story in the country there.'

We said, 'All right then.'

They said, 'Well, to put a land claim in we'll come out, record all the rock history and the Dreaming story, and the song. Then we go to the judge and we'll go to court about it. If we win, you've got the land.'

I said, 'All right, well go ahead.'

First we jumped on a plane and were flying around on top, showing them what the area looked like. Then second, we went across with the helicopter and landed in a few places, and I gave them a story about the sacred sites. Then I travelled around with them in a car to show them all the rocks with the story and the song. Then later on we brought Justice Kearney and the Conservation Commission and the government people—lawyer and Christ knows what else—and we started off from the Daly River at the Claravale Crossing, and we land-claimed it all around. I took them out and we started talking about all the history of the country, this Dreamtime history and songline, and I gave the name out to all the sites of the hills. Then we sang all sorts of songs for the judge to hear and he said, 'How did you know all that?'

I said, 'Well I was taught with my old stepfather. Old Joe Jomornji showed us all this.'

Judge Kearney he believed us and he said to me, 'For you, you've got no problem in this country. This is your land, you know the history of all the sites and everything—the story for the country. You can sit there, and I'll take that up.' Then he went back and told the pastoral property owner that we are allowed to stay there till the decision of the land claim will come through.

Anyway, after we finished, we went back to Katherine again, they dropped me off, and I headed across to DAA and I said, 'Look, I want to go down and live in the back of the Flora and wait for the land claim to come through.'

They said, 'All right, you can go there and sit down.'

First I rang up Luke Wise, the manager at Scott Creek Station where my land claim was, and at first he didn't want to know us—he just put the phone down. So I ended up going across to the Welfare and talking to a couple of blokes called John Rider and Bill Hearn and old Ted Tonkin, and next Ted Tonkin said, 'Take Bill to see the manager. He just wants a small living area,' so we jumped on a Toyota and went out to Scott Creek.

Luke Wise seen us coming and he stood there for a while by the office, and when we got closer he went into the office, and opened up the window and he put his head out. He said, 'Where are youse going to?'

'Oh,' we said, 'we want to go down and see if we can get started on this small block of land down on the Flora River, because it's part of our country. We only want a small bit.' Well, he slammed the door on us and he wouldn't come out of the office.

Then later Luke Wise sold Scott Creek to the Sultan of Brunei. We said, 'Well, new owner, we'll have another go,' and we just drove straight in on the south side of Scott Creek and we went down to the river. Then some of the blokes that worked around there saw us and next we can hear this helicopter coming all the way along the river, and it landed there. Marie Allan had a DAA vehicle in there, and the helicopter landed next to the DAA vehicle, and these blokes came down and said, 'What are you doing in here?'

We told him what we were going to do, that we were going to stay there, and they said, 'How long are you here for?'

I said, 'All my life, that's what I'm going to stay here for.'

They said, 'Get out.'

'Well,' I said, 'I'm not shifting. You'll have to come with the bulldozer and shift us. We belong to this country. We were reared and grown up in this country.'

They went back with a report and tried to get us out—ringing policemen and Christ knows who else to get us out. We had lots of rows, and they were aerial baiting all around the country to poison all the dingo, and they flew right over on top of us dropping poison meat, and killed some of our dogs. We came down and made a complaint with the Conservation mob and they were jumping up and down as well, and that sort of stopped them, and me and my family stayed over there then, not to be annoyed by these people.

Next, we had to wait a long while, till 1981. While we were waiting, my old mum, old Ludi, she died. I was going to take her out to the bush and bury her, but we had a bit of a blue with the Shire Council because they said you weren't supposed to take anybody out and bury them in the country. Also, the land claim was not finished, and the bloke at Scotts Creek stopped us. We finished up burying her in the cemetery in Katherine, and we were a little upset because we should have taken the old lady back and buried her in the country.

Anyway, we were just waiting and waiting for an answer on the land claim and one day I rang up the lawyer from the Land Council and I just blew him up. I told him straight, 'Look, how come this land claim is so slow?' I said, 'A lot of old boys are dyin' out waitin.' I said, 'I got a crook back too, and if we don't get it through I'll be dead and my young fellas wouldn't know what to do.' That's what I told them.

He said, 'Oh yeah, yeah,' but I got up him whether he liked it or not.

Well we waited all the way, then I get a telephone call and they said, 'Your land is claimed, it's going to be surveyed now. It's complete. Finished.'

'Well,' I said, 'that's my proper country now.'

But it's too late now, everything has been destroyed already, you know. The liquor, the Aborigine got destroyed by the liquor, waiting too long, trying to fight to go back to his land to live the traditional way. But the pastoralists kept on saying 'No, you can't go back,' and while they was saying that the younger people growing up in the town didn't know actual Aboriginal law, because they went the opposite way, into this booze and going to school. That school is all right, but going to the discos and not doing traditional ceremony, that destroyed a lot of culture. The older people were still alive around about that time when the booze come in, but because so many younger ones were coming in to the initiation place drunk, the old people said, 'No, don't let 'im in, he's interrupting a ceremony, we'll cut the initiation right off now.' They stopped it, but before grog we were keeping initiation all the way, right through, all the way right up until 1968.

But my boys are all right, because they were with me all the time in the bush, and I was teaching them about the bush food, the honey, and many different yams, and many different fruits on top of the tree, and all this sort of thing—but not in the actual traditional way like when I was brought up walking around with a cock-rag and a spear in our hand. But I'm teaching them about doing up the paintings and making boomerangs, and they are asking a question or two. But I'm a bit worried with the others because their parents are on the booze and they're not explaining anything to them much at all, you know.

But now the land has been handed over, the land Aborigine can explore, to control their sacred site, where they can give the young Aborigine the understanding about the bush tucker and the bush medicine and the initiation, and all the things that I learnt off old Joe Jomornji and my old grandfas. My boys have been initiated now, too, because we are getting back to the olden time now.

PART FIVE

OWN BUSINESS (1983 ON)

Chapter Twenty-four

TOP ALL 'ROUND

Anyway, we got our land back, and there was no more cattle work on the property—all the stockmen have finished up—and we were sitting down by the river, and I decided, 'Well, I can't sit here much longer, I must go over and work.' I made up my mind and I said, 'I'm gunna try and start myself a contract.'

See, I grew up in the Aboriginal camp, didn't know what the money was, then I was gettin' thirty bob a week, and I made huge amount of money for another company and I made none for myself. So I switched it around the other way and I came down to Katherine and I started off picking up beer cans. Then the Conservation people heard that I was a good yard builder and ideal to talk to people, and they had a mob of students from overseas, in 1985, and they said I might be good to give them a good understanding about the bush.

I said, 'Yeah, no worries.' Anyway, these students came along and I took them out in the bush, canoeing with the dinghies and showing them how to live the bush way—catching fish from the river and cooking them in the coal; making johnnycakes and feeding them with the bush honey—and all this sort of thing. They reckon that was great, they haven't seen anything like that, and it was very interesting for people from overseas. Lot of Americans, all different nationalities we had there. They really loved it see.

Then the Conservation Commission came across and they said, 'Look, we've heard about you building yards. Could you come along and install the yard at Bullita, it's a national park now.'

I said, 'Okay, I'll do that,' and I went over to King River, cut a lot of lancewood rails, and took them across.

They said, 'No shortage of labour, because you're going to teach all these young students who came across from overseas to build the yard.'

I said, 'Okay,' and I taught all them young lady and young boy students who came across from overseas, and we brought Bullita stockyard back to normal again.

Of course I was on the wages first, and at the same time they said, 'We can't give you wages for all the rails, what about can you give us a price of how much you want for the rails?'

I said, 'All right, $5 a rail.' Anyway, then I did the fence at Katherine Gorge, but the money started to build up a bit. Then John Fletcher from the Conservation Commission said to me, 'Old man, you must form yourself a small company, otherwise the tax man will get you.'

I said, 'Okay,' and then I went into the tax man. We formed a company called Colmara Pty Ltd, and started up as a fencing specialist, and we done a lot of heritage work with the fencing, all around the countryside.

Then the Tindal Air Force Base started up in '87 and they were asking for an Aboriginal organisation to build the fences. I went around and seen a bloke called Phil Harlow—he was the main big wheel in there with all these other government people, and they were very pleased for me to drop in and have a yarn to them about me doing all the fencing. 'Well,' they said, 'you can have all the fencing there that you want. Just go ahead and get us a quote for this.'

Of course I didn't know how to quote the job, but I had another bloke assist me with the first couple, and after that I never looked back. I put all those big fences in Tindal Air Force Base—the high perimeter fence, internal fence, radar fence and all that sort of thing—I put the whole lot in at Tindal. I'm well and truly in with the heads there. I go, sit down, I talk sense to them. They can see my work. Neat job. Good work, and I had fifteen blokes working for me. Then the last big fence that we did was the bombing range at the back of Delamere—it was a stock route—and there's 100 kilometres of fences at Delamere to stop the cattle going in.

At the same time one old bloke called George Chaloupka from Darwin came around to see me. He's very expert on the rock art paintings, and he said, 'The paintings 'round Wardaman country, too good to be left alone. Might be better if you could make a movie out of it so people could see it,' all the painting of the Lightning Brothers and my totem *bulyan* and everything else.

I said, 'Oh yeah, I suppose, but we have to have a yarn with the rest.' Then I went over and had a yarn with the other Wardaman people and everybody agreed, and they organised a film crew from Film Australia in Sydney, and they came down and did all the filming with us.

And while we were down there doing the filming we did the proper ceremonies for the spirit for my first wife, old Ida. We couldn't do it before because we couldn't go back to the country, but after the land rights it was all right. We sang the *yangalangi* song and put her spirit away. That was about seven years after she died till we got out there to do that, and now she can be reborn again.

Anyway, when the film was made they said to me, 'If it look any good, we'll call for you to come down to Sydney to launch the film.'

I said, 'Okay.'

Then when I was still working in Tindal, they phoned me. They said, 'You must come down to launch the film. We'll pay your fare and accommodation and everything. Come.'

I said, 'All right,' then I went to Sydney and they launched that film called *Land of the Lightning Brothers*, and I gave a talk in Sydney about the rock art, how Aboriginal people were living in the country, how we shelter where the rock art painting is, under the ledges of the rock. Over five hundred to a thousand people was there, and I talked to them. I wasn't scared, and the whole world saw the TV. The *Lightning Brothers* come on and everybody all over Australia saw the paintings, and now they realise why now the Aborigine wants to go back to actual land to live, to support their country with all these heritage sites.

The same time the mob in Tindal saw it come up on the screen and said, 'Well the fencing won't be able to last so long. Seems that there is a very good business in the tourism, and everybody doing it. Best you do it, because you got the history of the life in your painting.' They said, 'Go ahead, why don't you start up a tour?'

I said, 'Oh yeah, that sounds good to me,' and I was thinking about it for a long time. Then I thought again, I said, 'Well, maybe I do that because that way I can take people out in the art site, and give them the background and history of all the Aboriginal arts in the country.'

Of course I was shuffling around a bit first, and I was saying 'Oh well, how to go?' I headed across and seen Chris Burchett in Darwin at the Tourist Commission, and I talked to him about how I wanted to start up a tour.

First thing that Chris said to me was, 'Well, we've got to go down and have a look at the waterhole first, see if there are any bugs in it.' They came down and had a look at the waterhole, and he said, 'It's a good waterhole.' Now Chris said, 'You must get somebody who's been operating a tour before, you know, been a tour guide, to show you how to operate the tour.'

I said, 'No. I'll start off myself.'

Again he said, 'Well, you must have somebody who's been operating a tour and had a camp site built to set up your camp so you know what they're like.'

I said, 'No, I'll build it myself and you can come down and have a look.'

He said, 'Okay.' Then they checked on me to see if I was a good cook and a clean person, and they said, 'You capable bloke to start up your own tour. You can take off, any time.'

With the setting up of the camp, we headed across to see the consultant for the Sultan of Brunei and we said to them, 'Look, we want to go over and run the tour on Willeroo area, around Ingaladi.'

The bloke said to me, 'Well, we'd sooner see the tourist bus go in and not any other outsider. We are quite happy for you to go in.'

I said to him, 'Look, what I'll do, I'll make sure all the gates are closed when I go in. I make sure that no one throws a fire. I'll make sure that no one come in there without asking Willeroo. If they didn't know about asking at Willeroo, I'll chase them off. That's what I'll do.'

They said, 'Good on you.'

Then I came back and Chris helped me to promote the tour. We organised another bloke called Martin Libby in Darwin, and he set me up on the books side of the tourism, and we went down south to do the promotion, and when we come back we had the bookings. But when we had the booking we had no bus. We were shuffling around quick and got the money from somewhere—I only had $10 000. Anyhow, I put that $10 000 towards a bus, and I had to borrow money from ADC, then I bought an old bomb off Terra Safari and we started 'Bill Harney's Jankangyina Tour'—that's what he's called—to the Land of the Lightning Brothers. *Jankangyina* mean 'lightning man'. The first three or four people to come in on my tour were from Austria. They liked it, and from there it continued on, and it's still on there today.

Then the Tourist Commission said to me, 'You must come overseas and promote your tour.' First we went across to London, and I was very anxious to see London because Vesteys came from London. It's a very big city, they got lots of houses there, and we promoted the Aboriginal culture tour, and then we went across to Spain to a big meeting all about the tourism. They were very interesting people the Spanish people, and I seen them riding around with the horses in the main street—the town street so narrow like a corridor or the gorge in the country here—and on every corner I saw people playing guitar and dancing in the street to pick up a few bob. I saw homeless people over there, laying wrapped up with the blanket in the cold morning, under the palm tree. Some was curled up in the doorway and the bloke used to go along and boot them up the rib so they can open the door to get in, and this friend of mine on the tour, Brian Rook, we said to ourselves, 'God this is maybe worse than Australia. At least the Aborigine over there in Australia they have a friend who can offer them a place to sleep, they can get a feed and everything. But here it's all different. They have no friend of any sort!'

Then another time we went to Frankfurt and Berlin and we saw the same thing. The young kids screaming and shouting in the street, and the little German kids drunk as a monkey, and kids sitting down with a little hat, and everybody walking along dropping a coin to them. We felt very sorry for these kids. They were so homeless. We said, 'God! This is worse!'

Then later we went across to America. We did twenty-seven cities and we saw a different style there again. Lots of people say America is very rich, and some people might be rich all right, but there were lots and lots of homeless people in the country. We saw people walking around with a little container asking for any change, and we put some money in. Some people we saw in California were walking around with a trolley doing their street shopping for scraps in the rubbish bins. We said, 'God this is a different way, look at the really homeless people. We'd be too shy to do this in Australia.' On another corner we saw a group of white people sitting on a little park in a circle like the Aborigine in Australia all passing this one wine around, and Brian and I said to ourselves again, 'God! In Australia we can go down and get a drink of water. But in this big city they got to buy the water from the shop.' I never thought I'd go all over the world, but I did and it was good for me to see, so I could have it in my mind, and we talked to lots of people over there about the Lightning Brothers.

Now on my tours, lots of people asked me, 'Why did you start this?'

I told them, 'Well, if I didn't start this tourist business all of the history and the heritage wouldn't have been here. No one would know about it. I started this tourism to give youse a good history of all of the Aboriginal culture, what was in the past. I'm here if you want to know anything, I'm here to tell you all,' and everybody was pleased about it.

I do all the cooking for them—I make the damper, custard and all. The people say to me, 'Where did you learn to cook? You got a book or something?'

I say, 'No, I haven't got a book. When I was growing up as a kid we had so many different cooks in the property and I was watching them. We had some good cooks and some bad cooks, but I put all the cooks together, and that's why I'm dishing out this meal to you, to have a feed.' Anyway, they enjoy the feed and they reckon I'm a great cook.

Then I take them out to show them the country where there's lots and lots of Lightning Brothers painted in the rock, and many different creatures, kangaroos, dingoes, and I take them out to show them the man on the pack horse, and I say to them, 'This is the first lot of European that come into this country, and this is the picture of the policeman exploring for Aborigine, picking him up from the bush to become tame, so they could work in the property.'

And I think in our Wardaman country we got the best art site in the country. I heard a lot of people from Jabiru and all around Kakadu say there are huge painting sites around Arnhem Land, but up there you got mainly crocodiles and turtles and barramundi, but over here we got huge numbers of the Lightning Man. Our painting is 6 to 8 foot long, 2 metres high, big ones, and the tourists they're really rapt, they go mad over this Lightning Man.

Some people that I come across say they read in some history book and in some documentary from Japan that there might have been a spaceman around this country, and they reckon the spaceman look exactly like the Lightning Man on the painting, like a God man. Could've been a spaceman, I don't know. I just know we call them the Lightning Man, and I was taught that by old Joe Jomornji. I tell them how old Joe Jomornji was a painter and that's why I come to learn about painting, bush way, traditional way, on the rock. Old Joe and my uncles and grandfather taught us to paint, when we was a kid. They said, 'You can't touch this till you went through this law. When you get older, and we go, you can paint 'em.'

For this rock painting we got red ochre on the banks of the creek, and we got white ochre, and we got yellow ochre, and all I got to do is just mix goanna fat together with those paints and rub it into the rock, and the fat and the paint never come off. That's why the rock painting is still there today. But if you do this with the water it will peel off straight away in the rain. But cattle get in there sometimes and lick it off—must be the smell of the fat I suppose, and they're licking the salt that was in the fat. But before I go, before I die like, I'll give them a good touch up. There's about a couple of thousand painting sites in the country in the Wardaman land, you know, and before I go I'll just redo the whole lot, and that will last for another two or three hundred years.

And today now, I do the painting on the bark and the canvas. I think that's the best business, a good job. I should have started off with that early but I woke up too late, see. If I'd known I could get $4 000 a painting I wouldn't have been running around picking up beer cans! I thought the painting was just nothing. I didn't know it's big money. Anyway I was taught from me dad and my mum and grandfather and grannies all about the paintings. We used to cut the sapwood trees and strip the bark and then polish it up and we used to paint it. The first exhibition we had in Darwin, and the second one coming up again in Darwin, and the next one going to be at Melbourne. Should be all right then, yeah.

Today now I still got the fencing contract business, but I'm not working it—I'm hangin' on to it for one of the young boys to take off with it. One of them is very keen on the tourist side of things because I take him out on a tour and he listens to the story and learn about a rock art story and all that. That's Roderick, he's very keen on it, and he might be able to take over tourism when I keel up.

Again I got another young fella, Cedrick, from Dixie, he's six year old. I didn't put him to school yet, but I'm teaching him the Aboriginal way, about bush life and the

name of everything in the bush tucker line. He even asks
me what's the story of the country, and I give him a run-
down on all that, then at night-time he tells me the same
story—that means he's learning a lot. After that I'll take him
over to the European school. By that time he won't forget
the Aboriginal culture school what I give to him. I said if
I brought him to school first he'll forget about the bush
side, he won't listen to me, he'll listen to the other way.
The other two, Billy and Roderick, they were the opposite—when I chuck them over to school they were more
or less interested in the school side—play toys, climb up the
stairs and slide down the skid, swinging, running around,
play baseball, football, soccer and all sorts of things. But in
Aboriginal way it's different, totally different. You don't do
that. You show him how to paint and tell the story, and
that's what I been doin' to the young fella, Cedrick. The
other two picked it up only when they grown up, and now
I gotta teach them how to paint. They was taught in the
school about painting, but the European way, you know,
with waterpaint. That's why I'm teaching them bush painting, and they'll be good when they finish.

Anyway, to finish up, when I was a young fella I thought
everything was going to be the same in the country all the
way, but gradually things started to change, town developed,
the highway went up, sealed road all over the country. Everything is changed all over now. A lot of people in the bush
in the old days used to say 'Aboriginal people are useless'.
They said the Aboriginal couldn't read or write, that only
the white person could do these things. But we say the Aboriginal is not useless, because they know their jobs—shoeing
up the horse, making the hobbles, making ropes, the Aboriginal lady making the homemade soap, butter, and growing
the garden to keep the European going in the country, and
all these sort of things. If you went out bush and you got
lost, the Aboriginal would go about and find you, and look
after you with the bush food and make sure you get well
fed. We had this argument with the policemen. We said, 'If

you want to go out somewhere, you must take Aboriginal to guide you, eh?'

They said, 'Oh yeah, I never thought about it,' and then they realised we weren't useless at all.

As for me, I said to my boys, 'With my experience, all my life, I always get on well with all the businessmen, many of the managers, policemen, lawyer, everybody. I get on well with 'em because I talk sense, I don't talk any rubbish or grog talk, I talk really sense to everyone. Whatever they ask, I give 'em a good answer. Anyway, I don't want to see youse fall down and get a bad name, because I always had a good name myself. Look at me,' I said, 'I didn't go to school, your grandpa old Bill Harney he had the knowledge of everything and he wrote a book about what he saw, and he didn't go to school.' I said, 'He got on well with Aborigine, he left a good reputation behind, I picked it up, I got a good reputation, you gotta have a good reputation.' That's what I told the boys.

They said, 'Okay, we stick to that.'

And I said to Billy, 'I'm Bill Harney number two, and you are Bill Harney number three. We can't throw that name away. When you grow up and have another, you call him Bill Harney four. We got to carry that name on.' Now he's got a little baby, and he's Bill Harney number four.

And there's a lot of other kids come in and they stay with us because their mother is out in the disco or going around with different blokes all over the country, and the parents are split on the booze, and these kids know they can get a feed at my place. We take care of the kids and I don't have drink at all in my house. My house is very dry you know—none of us drink. I don't drink, my missus don't drink, and that's why we take a care of any kids that come. We're not getting any money out of it or anything—we're just looking after them, that's about all.

Well, from the beginning, I was born in the bush and growing up in the bush. First was the blackfella way. I was grown up with the story, right through till the time I moved into the

European camp, and then I saw the different lifestyle of the European, and I was brought up in the European camp. Now today I put the Aboriginal lifestyle and the European lifestyle together, and I know the both laws, because Joe Jomornji and all my uncles and grandfa and my mum taught me the Aboriginal law. All my grandparents and all my uncles have passed everything over to me, and there's only a few old fellas left like me now. We are the ones that have got the control over all the information that was passed from the old people. We are the leader for the Wardaman and have control of ceremony.

I haven't been to school, but I went to the university in the bush, under the tree, beneath the stars. The lifestyle I went through, I reckon it's fantastic. People will say of me, 'Well, he was a very good stockman, good horseman, good musterer, good for making ropes, hobbles, bullcart ropes, good at building yard fences, breaking in horse, operating the cattle—at all that, he's the man.' I don't know whether any other Aborigine would have brains as good as I got, but if someone has, well, he'd be a good man, he can ride right over me, because in my lifestyle I come out top all 'round.

GLOSSARY

ADC Aboriginal Development Corporation, a government body to assist Aboriginal people in business.

Bella Kriol for fella.

Blitz A light four-wheel-drive truck, specified by the US army, and manufactured mainly by the Chevrolet company. Many were auctioned after the Second World War for continued use in north Australia.

Bob (as in two-bob piece) Slang for two shillings in the currency before dollars and cents, equivalent to twenty cents.

Bogie A wash.

Bough shelter Upright posts, most often thin tree trunks, with leaves laid upon crosspieces for a roof, used in bush camps.

Brownie Cake baked on campfire, made from flour and water, and possibly treacle, sugar, sultanas and currants—whatever is available.

Bullwaddy *Macropteranthes kekwickii*, a tall tree that grows thickly in an east–west belt across the Northern Territory, marking the divide between the desert and the tropical country.

Conservation Conservation Commission of the Northern Territory.

CIB Criminal Investigation Branch (police).

Clap sticks Percussion instrument made of two wooden sticks.

Condamine bells Bells around a horse's or cow's neck. The Condamine is a river in Queensland.

Conkleberry *Carissa lanceolata*, a small shrub with a black berry and fine leaves.

Cooee A penetrating call—'Coo-ee'—for communicating over long distances in the bush.

Coolibah *Eucalyptus microtheca*, a gum tree common in inland areas subject to occasional flooding.

Corroboree General term for Aboriginal dance of non-sacred nature.

Donga Makeshift and transportable shelter.

DAA Department of Aboriginal Affairs, forerunner of the present Aboriginal and Torres Strait Island Affairs Commission.

Dreamtime/Dreaming A fundamental Aboriginal religious concept. Traditionally every Aborigine has a personal Dreaming that is usually a totemic figure, an ancestral creative being which is located at sites in his or her own country. But the Dreaming also described an entire world view—including the past, when everything was created, through the present and into the future—and represents the whole body of Aboriginal knowledge.

Drovers Horsemen and women who walk cattle from cattle stations to the railheads, abattoirs or markets.

Finger, money in the Money in the hand.

Fire-plough A large forked stick, A-shaped, pulled behind donkeys to plough a road or airstrip.

Gallon licence The licence that was given to a store or wayside shop to sell alcohol to take away.

Gammon An old English word popular with Australian Aborigines, meaning to pretend, deceive.

Gidgee trees Stinking wattle tree.

Goolie Stone.

Grandfa Mother's father.

Granny A male is called a granny when he is your mother's uncle. Otherwise a granny is your mother's mother.

Gunjimab A card game.

Hardy, Frank Author and unionist who was active in the Gurindji action. Wrote *The Unlucky Australians* (1968), which recorded the events.

Horse tailer The boy or man in the stock camp who rises at dawn to round up the horses for the day's mustering.

Inland Missionary A missionary from the Aborigines Inland Mission of Australia, an interdenominational (Protestant) mission that began in NSW in 1905, and went to the Northern Territory in 1936.

Johnnycakes Scones cooked on the coals, made from flour and water, or native bush seeds.

Kelly, Ned The most famous and celebrated Australian bush-ranger or rural outlaw.

Killer, a A bullock that is for eating.

Kriol Name of the creole language of north Australia, creole being the generic term for a new language that develops when two or more languages come into contact.

Lancewood scrub Lancewood is a tough, straight tree with elastic wood. Thick stands of lancewood can be impenetrable. The wood is ideal for bough shelters and stockyard rails because of its resilience to white ants and weather.

Lijarri *Gyrocarpus*, a pale-barked squat tree with helicopter-like seeds, otherwise known as Shitwood because the soft wood is useless for firewood or making spears. Used for carving into bowls and coolamons.

Narga A cloth, tied around the waist, and worn like under-pants. Otherwise called a cock-rag.

Never-never The country that is far away in the distance, no one in sight, silent, a void. An urban/coastal reflection upon the vastness of the Australian interior connected with the perception that the 'outback' is empty.

Northern Land Council The organisation set up under the 1976 Northern Territory Land Rights Act to represent Aboriginal claimants in land claims.

Pad Walking track.

Poddy-dodging Stealing cattle, particularly unbranded (clean-skin) calves.

Porcupine Actually an echidna, but the first English word European people gave Aboriginal people for that similar-looking animal was 'porcupine' and, naturally, it stuck.

Ringers Stockmen.

Rooting horses Horses that buck.

Scoot To 'go on the scoot' means to go on a drinking spree.

Scrubby Removed from the niceties of 'civilisation' as in 'living in the scrub and looking like it'.

Shilling Coin in the old currency—equivalent to ten cents.

Skin The name of groupings in the Aboriginal kinship system have been roughly translated as 'skin' groups, though each language group has their own name for these divisions.

Skin-graft Cutting the branded skin off a cow or horse and, when the skin has regrown, replacing the old brand with a new one.

Songline Coined by Bruce Chatwin in his book *Songlines*, Cape, 1987, songlines are epic creation songs which have been passed to present generations by a line of singers continuous since the Dreamtime. These songs, or song-cycles, have various names according to which language group they belong to, and tell the story of the creation of the land, provide maps for the country, and hand down law as decreed by the creation heroes of the Dreamtime. Some songlines describe a path crossing the entire Australian continent.

Station Cattle property.

Straight skin By the Aboriginal system of kinship, a man and a woman in the respective 'skin' groups that allow them to be husband and wife are said to have 'straight skin'. People marrying outside these groups, e.g. cousins, are considered to be 'wrong side'.

Strides Trousers.

Swag Bedroll consisting of canvas cover for mattress and blankets.

Swagstrap Leather strap for rolling swag.

Sydney Williams hut Prefabricated steel hut, made of angle iron and corrugated iron, and manufactured by Sydney Williams in Rockhampton, Queensland, also the manufacturer of Comet windmills. Sydney Williams huts first came to the Northern Territory in 1911.

Ten-bob note In the old currency, a ten-bob note was ten shillings, or half a pound.

Two bob A two-shilling coin revalued at twenty cents when decimal currency was introduced in 1966.

VRD Victoria River Downs Station.

Welfare A generic term given by Aborigines to all people who worked in the early days of 'welfare', whether it was officially known as Welfare or as the Native Affairs Branch.

Whitlam, Gough The Australian Prime Minister (1972–75)

whose government was responsible for the introduction of the 1976 Northern Territory Land Rights Act, although he did not survive in government to see it passed by Malcolm Fraser's Liberal government.

Yackai An exclamation, like yippee!

Yards Old imperial measurement of distance: one yard equals 0.9144 metres.

Yella fellas Term for people with mixed Aboriginal–European or Asian heritage, used by both black and white alike.

TEXT ACKNOWLEDGMENTS

The authors and publishers would like to thank the following individuals and organisations for their kind permission in allowing the material listed below to be reproduced on the page numbers given. Every attempt has been made to trace copyright holders of the material reproduced in this book, and the publishers would be pleased to receive any further information.

E.C. (Ted) Evans for extract from *The Moving Finger* (unpublished ms.), pp. 77–8.

Mrs Ruth Lockwood for extracts from *Harney's War* (W.E. Harney), pp. 12–13; *Life Among the Aborigines* (W.E. Harney), p. 37, pp. 143–4; *To Ayers Rock and Beyond* (W.E. Harney), pp. 155–6; *The Shady Tree* (W.E. Harney with D. Lockwood), p. 158.

Australian Archives, Darwin, for extracts from Report to the Native Affairs Branch by Patrol Officer W.E. Harney (June 1945), pp. 71–3; Report on Manbulloo, Willeroo and Delamere Stations to Native Affairs Branch from Patrol Officer E.C. Evans (22 August 1950), p. 95; Report on Manbulloo Station to Native Affairs Branch from Patrol Officer J.R. Ryan (26 February 1953), p. 114.

Australian Broadcasting Corporation, ABC Radio, for extract from *Harney's War* (1958), p. 12.

The Australian Meat Industry Employee's Union (Victoria Branch) for extracts from *The Vestey's Story* (Peter D'Abbs), p. 9 and pp. 123–4.

The Katherine Historical Society for extract from *The Katherine 1872–1917*, p. 45.

Katherine Times for the extract from 'Station Profile' by the National Trust NT (20 June 1985), p. 8.

INDEX